TO

Caroline Leigh

FROM

Gran

Easter 2023

i love you
with my whole heart

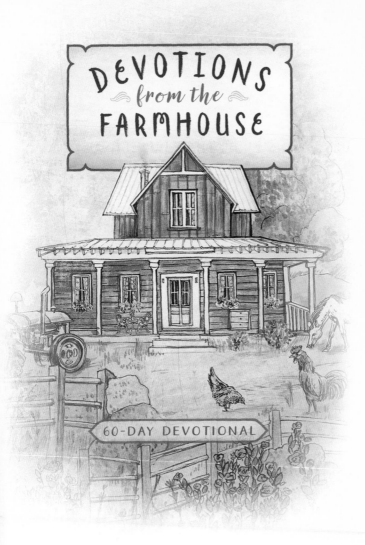

DEVOTIONS
from the
FARMHOUSE

60-DAY DEVOTIONAL

BroadStreet
PUBLISHING

BroadStreet Publishing Group LLC
Racine, Wisconsin, USA
Broadstreetpublishing.com

DEVOTIONS FROM THE FARMHOUSE

© 2017 by BroadStreet Publishing®

ISBN 978-1-4245-5575-8

Devotional entries composed by Michelle Cox and Linda Gilden.

Design by Chris Garborg | garborgdesign.com
Editorial services by Michelle Winger | literallyprecise.com

Printed in China.

17   18   19   20   21   22   23   7   6   5   4   3   2   1

Ask the animals, and they will teach you,

or the birds in the sky, and they will tell you;

or speak to the earth, and it will teach you,

or let the fish in the sea inform you.

Which of all these does not know

that the hand of the Lord has done this?

In his hand is the life of every creature

and the breath of all mankind.

JOB 12:7-10 NIV

INTRODUCTION

Sunrises are always beautiful. But not many are as gorgeous as the sun coming up over a farm pond. The pinkish orange glow rises over the trees and the world comes alive. The early morning quiet on the farm gives you time to ponder life as you watch the reflection of the landscape in the sparkling water.

As you spend time observing the cows, sheep, horses, wheat, carrots, potatoes, flowers, trees, birds, sky, or sun, remember to thank the Creator who made them all and put them in their place. Be encouraged as you spend time alone with God. May his peace and joy refresh you like cool water on a hot summer day.

GRANDPA'S FARMHOUSE

Remember the former things, those of long ago.
ISAIAH 46:9 NIV

Laney had wonderful memories of days she'd spent at her great-grandfather's old farmhouse. They'd shared many delicious meals there with platters piled high with Granny's fried chicken and biscuits. Laney remembered playing checkers on the porch with Grandpa, taking Sunday afternoon naps in front of the fireplace, and the laughter as uncles, aunts, and cousins played tag and ate Grandpa's famous hand-churned ice cream.

But the times that still made her tear up were the memories of the mornings she walked into the kitchen and saw her Grandpa reading his dog-eared Bible. The countless times he'd pulled her close and prayed for her with tears on his cheeks. The days when she'd hear Granny singing hymns as she worked in the kitchen. There was a sweet security in those moments.

Her great-grandparents had gone to heaven many years ago, but every time Laney walked through the front door of that house, warm memories wrapped around her as if Granny had draped one of her handmade quilts around her shoulders.

Laney's recollections of her grandparents were precious. When they died, they left her a little money and some gorgeous heirloom furniture that Grandpa had made, but Laney considered the best treasures were that they'd taught her by example about life, Jesus, and love.

What will your loved ones remember about you someday? Will they talk about a man or woman who loved God? Will they remember your faithful example? In the midst of your busy days, take time to live your faith in front of your family. That will be the most cherished inheritance you could ever leave them.

Lord, help future generations to remember me as someone who loved you. Help me to be faithful.

PLANTING PRECIOUS SEEDS

He who continually goes forth weeping,
Bearing seed for sowing,
Shall doubtless come again with rejoicing,
Bringing his sheaves with him.
PSALM 126:6 NKJV

I chuckled while I watched my little grandchildren
plant a garden in their backyard. Their seeds were
pretend ones and their tools were sticks they'd found at
the edge of the woods, but they were so excited about
the carrots and strawberries that would grow there
soon. Their enthusiasm brought back memories of
planting seeds when I was about their age.

My first gardening memory was at Granny and
Grandpa's house. Their food garden was huge, and
Granny bordered it with flowers that added a bright pop
of color during spring and summer. The results of their
labor were evident in their cellar which was packed with
canning jars filled with their vegetable bounty.

When I was about five, I finally got to help. I still
remember walking between the furrowed rows of dirt,

following Grandpa's directions as I dropped seeds into the holes. To my delight, I even got to plant my own potato patch.

I learned some things about planting seeds—crops don't grow unless we plant the seeds. We can't plant bean seeds and expect to harvest strawberries, and we can't plant corn and reap carrots. We reap what we sow.

That leads to the question: What kind of spiritual garden are we growing? That depends on what kinds of seeds we've planted, and how well we've tended our souls. A garden must be watered regularly and the weeds must be removed. The same is true of our hearts—and God promises that if we'll weep for others as we sow precious seeds, we'll reap a bountiful harvest.

※

Father, help me to sow seeds
that will matter for eternity.

IT'S NEVER IN VAIN

Be steadfast, immovable, always abounding in the work of the Lord, knowing that your labor is not in vain in the Lord.
1 CORINTHIANS 15:58 NKJV

Some days, Jake loved farming. There was no better feeling than looking out over his fields right before harvest. Leafy green corn stalks towered higher than his head. The tomato plants were so loaded that he'd had to tie them to stakes to keep them from toppling over.

There was a deep satisfaction in seeing the evidence of his labors, in enjoying fresh-from-the-field corn on the cob and ripe juicy slices of tomato with his dinner. Those were the good days.

But some years, it was anything but good. Those were the times when late frosts killed the strawberry plants, when the rains didn't come and the crops dried up, and when the locusts and other pests ate the profits right off the plants. Those were the days when he considered quitting. Times when he wondered why he did what he did.

Sometimes it's the same way spiritually. It's a pleasure serving Jesus when everything is going well, when the blessings are plentiful, and life is easy. But when hard times come, when discouragement sets in, and our finances dry up, we consider quitting. We wander away from what was once precious to us.

But just as a love for farming is in the blood of the farmer and that keeps him going year after year, we must remain steadfast because of the One who loved us enough to shed his blood for us. Whatever we do for Jesus will never be in vain.

✻

Lord, encourage my heart when tough days come.
Help me to serve you in good times and in bad.

AN ENCOUNTER WITH BEES

Take up the whole armor of God, that you may be able to withstand in the evil day, and having done all, to stand.
EPHESIANS 6:13 NKJV

Albert was excited about his new beehive. A beekeeper friend from church, Bob, helped Albert set up his hive, and then he guided the bees he'd brought for Albert into their new home. Bob shared valuable information about handling the honey bees and gave Albert instructions about what to do, but he was so mesmerized watching the bees that he didn't hear half of it.

A few days later, he went out to tend to the bees. He donned his bee suit, put the helmet and veil over his head, and slipped on the gloves. Albert walked up the hill to the hive and removed the top. He worked for a few minutes and then let out a bloodcurdling yell.

When his wife looked out the window, she saw him running down the hill towards the creek with a cloud of bees following him. Getting in the water helped him lose them, but he didn't escape unscathed. You see,

he hadn't listened to the instructions, and he'd put the bee suit on incorrectly. The bees had gotten inside the veil and his clothes, stinging him as he tried to escape.

Not listening well to the instructions caused a painful situation for Albert, and not listening to God's instructions can cause pain for us as well. Reading our Bibles and listening for God's voice will shield us from getting stung by situations that will harm us. And just as wearing the bee suit properly would have protected Albert, wearing God's armor of righteousness will protect us.

Lord, help me to listen to your instructions
and to wear your armor well.

DON'T MISS THE MOMENTS

Be still, and know that I am God.
PSALM 46:10 NKJV

There's a beauty to farm life if one slows down long enough to enjoy it. A simple joy lies in watching the changes in the fields: from being covered in snow in the winter to those moments weeks later when the dirt is turned over ready for a new crop. There's the sweet satisfaction of those first tender green shoots popping from the ground, and then watching over the next few months as squash, broccoli, green beans, tomatoes, and corn become ready for the family dinner table.

There's the delight in spending time in the fields with your family. Working side by side. Teaching the little ones the ins and outs of life on the farm, and skills that have often been passed down for generations.

What could be more peaceful than sitting beside the creek listening to the bubbling water or watching your cows as they munch grass in the pasture? Or sitting on a hillside enjoying the view as a tractor or baler makes

its way through the fields? Those are priceless moments that we often miss in the busyness of our days as we rush from one thing to the next.

The same is often true of our moments with God. He's provided us with opportunities to spend time with him as he shares his heart and wisdom with us—but we're usually too busy. It's those "be still" moments when we slow down that we truly enjoy the farm, and it's those "be still" moments with him when we hear his whispers to our hearts and enjoy the beauty of time spent with him.

※

Lord, help me to slow down so I don't miss the moments with you.

GOOD BYE, CRIP

The body does not consist of one member but of many.
1 CORINTHIANS 12:14 ESV

"Amen," Grandma said.

A round of "amens" followed and everyone silently walked up the hill. The funeral was well thought out, planned by the grandchildren. The deceased was Crip, a six-week-old chicken.

Even the animals are special to farm families. Not all receive a funeral at their passing, but Crip was like a member of the family. Born with a splayed leg, Crip lived inside and was pampered and played with every day. He responded when you called his name and loved for you to rub his back. But even all that love and care couldn't pull him through.

So the seemingly (to the grandchildren) fitting thing to do was to bury him in a special place on the farm. His grave was complete with duct tape tombstone and flowers, and he had a funeral that would rival many others.

Crip provided life lessons to the grandchildren, but he reminded the whole family that God loves and cares for all his creations. To some he might have seemed like a poor, crippled, cast off chick that couldn't walk, but he remained a special part of God's family and the farm family.

God doesn't look at any of his creation as insignificant. He created everyone for a purpose.

Some days you may not feel very significant and wonder about your purpose. God is waiting for you to ask him for guidance. He has a plan just for you. As Paul stated in our daily verse, each of us is an important part of the body of Christ.

Never think you are insignificant. Stand tall and step out to fill your God-created spot in the world.

※

Lord, thank you that I am important to your Kingdom.

NOT ON MY WATCH

"Be strong and of good courage, do not fear nor be afraid of them; for the Lord your God, He is the One who goes with you. He will not leave you nor forsake you."

DEUTERONOMY 31:6 NKJV

The farm animals were restless. Nervous whinnying came from the paddocks. Plaintive moos were heard from the pasture. The dogs barked. Even the cat flitted from window to window in the house. This was the kind of restlessness the farmer, Zeke, had experienced before when a tornado blew through the area or a bear, bobcat, or mountain lion wandered through the farm.

Since the weather forecast indicated calm weather, he knew it had to be a predator of some kind. Zeke armed himself, and walked outside and took stock of all the animals. Then he settled in a chair with his back to the barn door, a place where he could sit and see all the livestock that needed his protection.

A few hours later, he heard what sounded like a woman screaming—the cry of the mountain lion.

He could tell it was close. But he was armed and ready. No lurking predator would harm one of those defenseless animals while on *his* watch!

God also sees when dangers are waiting for us. He hears our restless murmurs. His ears are tuned to our cries and he recognizes each one. Whenever those moments arrive in our life, we have his promise that he will be with us, he is armed and ready, and we have no reason to fear. We can rest assured that *nothing* can harm us while on his watch.

Father, thank you for the security of knowing that you are watching over me. Thank you for never leaving or forsaking me.

PREPARING FOR WINTER

Go to the ant, you sluggard!
Consider her ways and be wise,
Which, having no captain,
Overseer or ruler,
Provides her supplies in the summer,
And gathers her food in the harvest.

PROVERBS 6:6-8 NKJV

A chilly wind whipped across the pasture. Cole could feel the moisture in the air. The first blizzard of the winter would arrive in a few hours, and newscasters said it was going to be a doozy, so Cole was preparing for the storm.

He put extra food and water out in the stalls for the horses, and did the same in the chicken coop. Cole drove the truck into the pasture and threw out extra bales of hay so the cattle could eat. And then he tied a rope from the house to the barn so he could get there to check on the animals even when the snow was blowing so hard that he couldn't see. He was prepared for winter.

Our verse today describes how the ant works steadfastly to gather food and supplies so it will be ready when winter arrives. We need to do the same thing for our souls. Before those "winter" moments arrive—the scary health diagnosis, the prodigal child, the unexpected job loss—we need to prepare. The verses you memorize during good days will be the ones that will sustain you during difficult ones. The stories about God's faithfulness that you've read so many times that you know them by heart will be the ones that will comfort you. And the close relationship you've built with God through prayer will give you strength.

Prepare now so you'll be ready when the winter seasons of life come your way.

Father, help me to prepare spiritually so that I'm strong and ready whenever I encounter difficult days.

THE BEST PLACE ON THE FARM

Come, let us bow down in worship,
let us kneel before the LORD our Maker.

PSALM 95:6 NIV

Stan loved everything about his farm—the house that his great-great-grandfather had built, the beauty of the land, and the bubbling creek that meandered beside the field.

But there was one place on the farm that was Stan's favorite. At the top of a gentle hill several hundred yards from the farmhouse, there was a small clearing at the edge of the woods. Stan had built a rustic bench there. This spot gave the perfect vantage point to look out over the farm, to see the blessings God had given him. He'd climbed that hill many times, sat there awhile, and returned to his work with his spirit refreshed.

The reason that Stan considered this the best place on the farm was that this was his prayer spot, where he went to be alone with God. There was something special about reading his Bible while surrounded by

God's creation. His family teased him about his off-key voice, but up there, Stan could sing songs of worship, a joyful sound to the God who made him.

He'd spent so many hours in prayer kneeling in front of that bench that there were grooves in the wood where his arms had rested while he prayed. This was Stan's place of power, for it was in that spot that he poured his heart out to God, where he got answers for his problems, and where he felt God's presence in a special way.

Sometimes it's hard to carve moments out of our busy days to spend time with God—but just as Stan discovered—the benefits are priceless.

Father, thank you for the gift of spending time with you.

THE STATE FAIR

A man's heart plans his way,
But the LORD directs his steps.
PROVERBS 16:9 NKJV

Four-year-old Josie was excited about showing her sheep, Wooly, at the State Fair. Her parents helped her practice walking down the country road with Wooly on a halter. They had trial runs of what to do when the judges came by to inspect the sheep.

They bathed and groomed Wooly until she was ready for her appearance at the fair. On the big day, Josie's group was called into the ring. She was cute as could be wearing her pink cowgirl boots as she walked Wooly around the circle. But there was one problem: That sheep was larger than that little cutie and it had a mind of its own—a rebellious mind.

That led to some problems for Josie. Instead of her being in charge, the sheep was in control of her. Where the other participants walked smoothly around the ring showing their sheep to the judges, Wooly pulled little

Josie wherever it wanted to go. She'd planned where she wanted to walk, but the sheep was directing her steps. The judges finally had to come help her get control.

It's the same way when it comes to serving God. So often, we have our plans all laid out. We know where we want to go and what we want to do—but we don't ask God what he wants us to do. Or worse, we know what path God wants us to take, and we rebel, striding off to achieve what we've planned instead of what he wants.

But just as Josie learned at the fair when the judges had to help her control her sheep, it's always wiser to let someone bigger be in charge.

※

Lord, help me to follow your steps.

TELL YOUR CHILDREN

*One generation shall praise Your works to another,
And shall declare Your mighty acts.*
PSALM 145:4 NKJV

There's a gorgeous farm tucked back in a mountain cove. The sloping fields dotted with cows provide a peaceful scene to those driving down the country road. The lush green grass and the bubbling stream have provided the Cooper family with a great place to farm.

Their great-great-grandfather purchased the 200 acres many years before. His children had worked in the fields with him. They had no other choice. It was either do that or go hungry, but they'd all ended up with a love for the land—one they'd passed on to their children.

And six generations later, the Cooper family still planted crops and raised cattle there, teaching their children the skills they'd learned from previous generations. Each year as they finished the harvest, they continued a special tradition. Their entire family would gather on hay wagons and ride to a remote place on the

farm for a picnic where the original family cabin still stood.

That was the day family stories were shared, the ones their great-great-grandparents had told about the hardships of their first winter in that cabin, about the years the crops failed, and the day Great-Grandpa Cooper had faced off with a bear. But most importantly, they shared stories about God's faithfulness, of how he'd provided all they needed, of how he'd been with them through good times and through bad.

Have you told *your* children your family stories? Have you shared with them about your faithful God and what a special place he holds in your life? The stories you tell today are the ones that will be repeated to future generations.

※

Father, help me to tell my children and grandchildren about your faithfulness.

ON THE LOOSE

"The Son of Man has come to seek and to save that which was lost."

LUKE 19:10 NKJV

Ellen's neighbor called, "Your cows are out." Ellen threw on her mud boots. Her husband seemed to have a gift for being gone whenever the cows got loose. She knew that the cows could get lost or hit by a car, or they could damage something, so time was of the essence.

Ellen called her mom who also lived on the farm. "Meet me on the road. Our cows are out."

The two women finally found them and then chased cows for what seemed like forever. Two went back in the fence pretty easily, but the other two were just ornery. They'd almost get one inside the gate, then it would bolt away at the last minute. And then they realized that the other cow was tromping on their garden, leaving mayhem and destruction behind.

Friends, it's often the same way with us. God has given us perimeters—fences—to protect us and to keep

us where he wants us. But sometimes we're just like those cows, we get minds of our own and we head away from his safety, being just as ornery as he tries to draw us back to him. It's for our own good, but we bolt away from him.

When we wander away from God, we become lost from his presence, we're susceptible to harm, and we damage our testimonies, relationships, and families. The good news is that—just like Ellen and her mom did with those cows—God searches for us. We are valuable to him, and he'll draw us back to his safe care . . . if we'll let him.

Lord, help me not to wander away from you.

FOLLOW ME

"My sheep hear My voice, and I know them, and they follow Me."
JOHN 10:27 NKJV

Jed had lived on the family farm for sixty-seven years. He was familiar with every inch of it, knew where the crops would grow best, what month the creek would dry up, and when the rooster would crow each morning. Farming had been a good life, often full of hardships and uncooperative weather, but also filled with blessings such as the cozy farmhouse that had echoed with laughter and the noise of a loving family.

He knew he was a rich man in every way that truly mattered, and he loved what he did. That included his livestock. It was a huge family joke that Jed had named every animal on the farm—quite a feat with thirty cows, fifty sheep, twenty chickens, ten pigs, and a menagerie of dogs and cats. He talked with them each day as he went about his duties on the farm, calling them by name, "Buttercup, how're you doing today, girl?"

Or "Fluffy, how much longer are you going to wait before you have those kittens?"

It was fascinating to watch him each evening as he walked out to the far pasture. The minute the sheep heard his voice, they started running to him, following him out of the gate. "Good evening, Lambie. Rambo, have you behaved yourself today? Rebel, c'mon now, cooperate. I've got to get back to the house." He knew them all, and he loved them.

We have a Shepherd who knows and loves us as well. We'd be wise to follow the example of those sheep in Jed's field—to listen for our Shepherd's voice, and to follow him wherever he leads us.

Lord, I'm awed that you know my name.
Help me to follow you.

I WILL STILL PRAISE YOU

Though the fig tree may not blossom,
Nor fruit be on the vines;
Though the labor of the olive may fail,
And the fields yield no food;
Though the flock may be cut off from the fold,
And there be no herd in the stalls—
Yet I will rejoice in the Lord,
I will joy in the God of my salvation.
HABAKKUK 3:17-18 NKJV

Levi's shoulders drooped in discouragement. Dry vegetation crunched under his boots—dry vegetation that should have been flourishing crops. It had been a devastating year. A late frost had wiped out their potential income from the peach trees. A storm with strong winds had ruined the corn crop.

And, now, the lack of rain had dried up the fields. He'd literally watched the plants wither and die, his hope dying with them. There would be no hay for the cattle. He'd already sold half of his herd because he wouldn't be able to feed them. Levi wondered how he'd

feed his family since there were no fruits or vegetables to can or to put in the freezer.

He kicked at a clod of dirt as he muttered, "God, what am I going to do? How am I going to provide for my family?"

And then he heard a quiet whisper in his soul, "Child, have I ever failed you before? Trust me. I will take care of you and your needs."

A sweet peace flooded Levi's heart. He didn't know how God was going to provide for them, but he knew with certainty that he was *able* to do it. And despite trees that didn't yield fruit, the lack of crops, and empty stalls in the barn, Levi was able to say, "No matter what, I will still praise you."

✤

Father, help me to praise you.

GRANDPA'S FISHING POND

Their children will be mighty in the land;
the generation of the upright will be blessed.
PSALM 112:2 NIV

Everyone wants to go fishing in Grandpa's farm pond. He stocks the pond each year with bass and bream, and most who are lucky enough to fish there have a good catch. Grandpa loves to share his pond and the joy of his fishing habit with others. However, he has one rule that you must follow if you come fishing there— you must bring a child with you.

Grandpa knows the benefit of spending time with someone of another generation, and he knows how much it means to have a companion for fishing. Many of the young boys and girls who fish in Grandpa's pond are fishing for the first time ever.

When you hold a fishing pole in your hand, you are prone to talk about whatever is on your mind, and often that opens doors for deep conversation. Children learn a lot about "way back then" and the older fishermen

learn about things that matter to the current generation.

Many families today are blessed to have four or even five generations, each with something to offer the others. What a treasure to be able to sit at the feet of a grandpa or great-grandpa and hear stories of "the good ole days."

Even better to share how God has cared for and grown people you know and love. Before the days of electronics, storytelling was a popular entertainment. That's how people learned, and that's how faith was shared.

Perhaps there is someone of another generation with whom you need to share your life. Your testimony of God's goodness will encourage others to follow him.

※

*Lord, help me to share the wisdom
you've given me with others.*

JUST KEEP ON

Let us not grow weary while doing good,
for in due season we shall reap if we do not lose heart.
GALATIANS 6:9 NKJV

Will didn't want to get up when his alarm clock went off. The week had been rough. He'd spent two late nights in the barn waiting for calves to be born and he'd had some long days out in the fields. The record-breaking heat hadn't helped matters any. He was weary. His body said, "Stay in this nice comfy bed!" but he'd cut hay the day before and he knew he had to bale it before the expected rain arrived late that evening. If the hay was ruined, his cattle wouldn't have enough to eat for the winter. He knew he had to just keep on going even though he didn't feel like it.

But he had a nice surprise when he got to the barn. His dad was waiting there. He'd seen his son's weariness the day before, and he'd come to help him with the hay. He stayed until every bale was in the loft.

Friends, we often experience something similar

in our lives. God asks us to do a task or he puts a big dream on our hearts. We work hard to make it happen, sometimes wearing ourselves out in the process. We don't see the end in sight, and we don't know how we're going to accomplish what God's asked us to do.

But just as Bart's dad came to help him get the hay up, we can count on our Father to be there with us, equipping us, encouraging us, and walking with us every step of the way.

Father, some days I'm weary and discouraged.
Help me to remember that a harvest lies ahead.

A FAITHFUL FARMER

Only fear the Lord and serve Him in truth with all your heart; for consider what great things He has done for you.
1 SAMUEL 12:24 NASB

The blizzard had raged for days, and it was several days after that before we finally dug out enough to get to the grocery store. The sight that greeted us when got there was unsettling. Delivery trucks had been stranded on the interstates, so no food had been delivered to the store in more than a week. The shelves were empty. The produce department only had a few stray items such as peppers and radishes. The meat counter shelves looked like a ghost town.

It was a visible reminder of how we depend on delivery trucks, and an even bigger reminder of how we depend on farmers—because without farmers, those food shelves would be empty every day. The meat department would be vacant. Our babies wouldn't have milk, and our dinner tables would be bare. Because of a faithful farmer's hard work and sacrifice, the rest of us get to eat.

In much the same way, we as Christians get to feed the gospel to the rest of the world. If we aren't faithful to give our dollars, to pray, and to get physically involved in mission trips and helping others, then hearts will be empty. Let's determine that we will work hard, pray hard, and tell of his sacrifice for us. Because wouldn't it be a shame for others to never get a taste of the most wonderful news in the world?

Lord, there are millions of hungry souls, people who need to hear about you. Help me to be faithful so that others will get a taste of your mercy and grace.

STRATEGIC PLANTING

That they may be called oaks of righteousness,
the planting of the Lord, that he may be glorified.
ISAIAH 61:3 ESV

My dad was in the garden planting the seeds he had chosen for this year's crops. Dad had prepared the soil with the tractor and cultivator, but when it came to the planting process, he always insisted on putting the seed in himself. He knew there were many devices and machines for dropping the seeds in nice straight rows as you make the furrows. He actually tried one. But for this farmer, the most important process of the garden is making sure you get the seeds right where you want them. "Do a little extra work now and you won't have to break your back thinning the little plants later!" he'd say.

Have you ever considered you might be in just the spot God has planted you? We may become dissatisfied with what is going on in our lives. We might feel like we have no purpose in what we are doing. But as believers, we can be sure that we are exactly where God wants us

if we have given him control of our lives. We may have struggles, but as long as we rely on him, God will help us push through the weeds of life.

We may not always see his plan as it unfolds but we can be sure he has the big picture in his control. As we bloom in the spot he has placed us, we can feel secure knowing the Master Gardener has carefully cultivated the land and dropped our seed exactly where he wants it to bloom.

Lord, help me to rest in knowing that you have put me exactly where you want me so that I can become a lovely flower in your garden.

PRESERVING THE CROPS

Teach the older women to...teach what is good. Then they can urge the younger women to love their husbands and children...to be busy at home, to be kind.

TITUS 2:3-5 NIV

Preserving the crops each year was a lot of work, but it sure tasted good on cold winter days when nothing fresh was growing. The skills to preserve food had been passed down for generations. Marsha had been quite young, but she still remembered watching Great-Granny Burleson as she dried slices of apple in the sunshine between two screens, and preserved pole beans by stringing them with a needle and hanging them up to dry. She'd called them "leather britches" and they'd looked like dozens of tiny green pants legs sticking out on the strings.

Marsha's great-grandmother taught her grandmother how to can food by using a boiling water bath and a pressure cooker to remove any bacteria and to seal the jar lids. She showed her how to cream corn,

cook it, and cool it in ice water before the containers went in the freezer. Those skills had been passed down to Marsha's mom, then to her, and now Marsha was teaching her own daughters.

God set up the plan for older women to teach the younger women. That goes back to Bible days. We've learned what to do—and what not to do—from our life experiences. We can share with others about how God was faithful to us, about what he taught us, and what we've harvested from his Word. Just as those farm women preserved their food, we can preserve the skills, knowledge, and faith God's given us and hand those down to future generations.

Lord, help me to share what you've taught me with my children and grandchildren.

LOOKING FOR LABORERS

"The harvest is plentiful, but the workers are few.
Ask the Lord of the harvest, therefore,
to send out workers into his harvest field."
LUKE 10:2 NIV

Roy could tell that this year was going to yield
the best harvest he'd ever had. The peach tree limbs
were drooping from the weight of the fruit. There was
a bumper crop of beans and squash. The corn was
the prettiest he'd seen in years, and there would be
hundreds of bushels of tomatoes to send to the market.

You'd think he would be excited, and he was, but
his biggest emotion was worry. The *Farmer's Almanac*
predicted major storms for the next few weeks, the kind
that would bring heavy winds and hail that would ruin
the crops.

He and his family had spent long days in the fields,
but they weren't making a dent with all that needed
to be harvested. He usually hired college kids or teens
from church to help, but this year, many of them

had internships or they were gone on mission trips for several weeks. He'd hung signs on local business bulletin boards and posted on social media that he was looking for laborers, but there were few responses.

God is also looking for some good laborers. There are people all over the world who are waiting for someone to bring them the gospel—a harvest of souls for God—but so few people are answering his call. We often think about foreign missionaries when we read this verse, but there are people all around us who need to hear about God's love. Will you be one of his laborers today?

Father, remind me that there is a plentiful harvest of souls. Help me to be one of your faithful laborers.

STRINGING BEANS

When you shall eat of the fruit of your hands,
You will be happy and it will be well with you.
PSALM 128:2 NASB

Laughter drifted from the porch of the farmhouse as the Anderson family strung and snapped green beans. A bushel was scattered across the tabletop and more bushels waited on the floor.

Even though she was just a teenager, Hannah had years of experience stringing beans. She'd had to do it by herself before and it was no fun. She could have sworn that somebody kept adding beans to the basket while she wasn't looking, because it seemed like no matter how much she'd done, the pile never diminished. And on the days when her attitude was bad, the job seemed even worse.

It was much more fun doing it as a family. Hannah knew she'd always have precious memories of those days. Moments of hearing Grandpa's stories from when he was a little boy. Hearing her little brother telling jokes

with a snaggle-tooth smile. Watching her dad and mom race to see who could string their beans the fastest. Enjoying the sweet harmony that wafted around them like country surround sound as they sang hymns of praise and worship. And listening to her daddy's prayer at the end of the evening, "Lord, we thank you for our family and for the blessings that you've given us."

Those were times of cherished fellowship, of enjoying the satisfaction of hard work, and of thankfulness for the success of their labors. And they were a great reminder that sometimes our biggest blessings can't be counted by the numbers in our bank accounts, but in the riches of the moments God gives to us each day.

Lord, thank you for our family and for the abundance of blessings that you've given us.

THE CHRISTMAS TREE FARM

God so loved the world that He gave His only begotten Son, that whoever believes in Him should not perish but have everlasting life.

JOHN 3:16 NKJV

Matt loved his job as a Christmas tree farmer. He had to wait longer to harvest the results of his labors, but that was okay with him. He enjoyed watching the trees grow each year, seeing them flourish from a foot high to tall beauties that would grace the homes of families for Christmas.

He took pride in trimming the young trees so that they would be beautiful and full when they were mature. The highlight for him came during those weeks from Thanksgiving to Christmas when families came to his farm. It made him smile to hear their laughter as clad in colorful coats, hats, and gloves, they rode out to the fields on the wagons, cups of hot chocolate clutched in their hands.

He loved helping them load their trees, knowing

that what he'd grown would become part of their family Christmas memories as they decorated it. But this year, the most exciting thing ever had happened. One of his Frasier firs had been chosen to stand in front of the state capitol where it would be decorated and lit up so everyone could see it. The tree had been Matt's gift and the state officials were happy to accept that.

God also decorated a tree in a public place—a cross—with the best gift ever: Jesus. The Light of the World who would shine into our lives with love, grace, and mercy. A gift that he freely gave so that we could have eternal life. And all we have to do is accept it.

Lord, thank you for decorating a tree so that we could have eternal life.

CITY SLICKER FARMERS

"Nor do we know what to do, but our eyes are upon You."
2 CHRONICLES 20:12 NKJV

Darrin and Frank built houses in the same subdivision, one that had acreage and was out in the country. Both had grown up in the city, and they were excited about the prospects of becoming farmers. There was one big problem, though—neither of them had any experience.

The two friends worked hard digging post holes and erecting a new fence. The two calves they brought home were adorable, but both had to be bottle-fed. That was quite an eye-opening experience for those two busy guys who'd never had to be responsible for farm animals before, and they didn't know what to do when they had trouble getting the calves to eat.

They set up a chicken coop at Darrin's house. The two men were disappointed when the hens didn't lay eggs for many weeks. Frank's wife had a little fun by dyeing some eggs and hiding them in the coop for the

guys to find one day. But the official egg deposits just weren't happening.

Darrin and Frank had one disappointment after another on their farm, and it was for one simple reason: They didn't know what they were doing and they didn't ask for help.

I suspect that many of us are just like Darrin and Frank. We set out to do something we don't know how to accomplish, but we don't ask God for help before we do it—and then we end up in a mess. Life would be so much simpler if we'd go to him for input first and then take action after that. Keeping our eyes on him is a great way to avoid mistakes.

※

Lord, help me to look to you
whenever I need help or guidance.

FIRST-FRUITS FARM

*Honor the LORD with your wealth, with the firstfruits of all
your crops; then your barns will be filled to overflowing.*
PROVERBS 3:9-10 NIV

Visitors flocked to the roadside stand, lured by the
nostalgic beauty of the old shed and the quality of the
produce. The setting looked like a painting. Loaves of
strawberry and zucchini bread lined the countertops.
The shed was filled with an abundance of ripe
strawberries, bins piled high with juicy watermelons,
and baskets of squash, peppers, and tomatoes.

Cooper and Ann had struggled for many years as
they farmed. The feast or famine lifestyle was hard. Late
at night during one of those difficult years, the couple
talked about what they were going to do. Ann said,
"We've talked about the situation a lot, but we've haven't
prayed about it nearly as much. We want to take care
of our family, but we both have always wanted to tithe
and give to missions as well. Let's start praying together
every night and ask God for ways that we can do that."

A few weeks later, God gave them the idea for the roadside stand. They named it "First-Fruits Farm" and determined that they would honor God with what they made there. Over the next twenty years, God answered their prayers beyond their wildest dreams, and they'd been blessed to pay for building wells in Haiti, to provide Christmas dinner for an orphanage in Africa, and to help elderly families from their church.

They discovered two things that will be of benefit to all of us: It's impossible to out-give God, and praying about our problems is far better than whining about them.

Lord, remind me to bring my petitions before you,
and help me to honor you with the first-fruits
of all that you give me.

AT THE STOCKYARDS

"You did not choose Me but I chose you, and appointed you that you would go and bear fruit, and that your fruit would remain."

JOHN 15:16 NASB

The sounds of mooing surrounded Clint as he walked through the stockyard. This was one of the busiest weeks of the year there, and it provided a great opportunity to choose the best stock for his herd.

He paused to look at the registered bulls. The purebred angus were beautiful, and it was evident they'd been pampered since birth. He knew that to become registered, they'd been weighed the day they were born, and a log had been kept since then. He always enjoyed looking at these bulls, but at $40,000-$50,000 each, they were out of range of his wallet.

Clint didn't choose his new cows without a lot of thought. He looked for good stock, checking the age, cleanliness, and muscle tone for each cow. He made sure there were no deformities, and no infections or

pink eye. He checked their build to see if they were well defined and that their weight was good for their age. Clint went for the best when he chose his cows and paid his hard-earned dollars for them.

I'm so glad that God didn't choose like that. He looked at mankind and was overwhelmed with love for us. He saw all our flaws and imperfections. He knew that he'd have a lot of cleaning up to do before we were of value. He saw that some of us were ornery and bullheaded and would take extra work. But he said, "I'll take that one . . . and that one . . ."

He said, "I choose *you*."

❋

Father, thank you for choosing me in spite of my flaws.

AN EXTRA CHAIR AT THE TABLE

With goodwill doing service, as to the Lord, and not to men, knowing that whatever good anyone does, he will receive the same from the Lord.

EPHESIANS 6:7-8 NKJV

Thelma had cooked lunch for the farmhands since she was a little girl standing on a chair helping her mama. Now she did the same for the workers who helped at her family's farm. A good hot meal would give them the strength and energy they needed for a long afternoon in the fields.

Some people would consider that cooking a large meal each day was drudgery, but Thelma saw it as a privilege. She hummed as she stirred the potatoes and sliced the roast. She cared about what she did and the people she served.

People loved eating at Thelma and Bert's house. The food was better than any restaurant and the welcome was even finer. Thelma always kept an extra chair at the table in case anyone else showed up—and they usually

did. Her warm hospitality fed the heart.

Friends, we can all set an extra chair at our table. It doesn't have to be a home-cooked meal, but there are people all around us who are hungry for someone to care about them, someone who will make them feel welcome. Sometimes we hold back from doing that because we don't have a fancy home or our house isn't spotless—but God says for us to serve others as if we were doing it for him.

Ask God to put someone on your heart today to fill that extra chair at your table.

Lord, help the welcome mat to always be out at my house. Give me the gift of hospitality so that others may experience your love.

TWO FARMS

All hard work brings a profit,
but mere talk leads only to poverty.
PROVERBS 14:23 NIV

There were two big farms on the country lane. Both had been handed down for generations. Hank's father had taught his son a good work ethic. Hank worked hard in the fields, tending his crops with care. He maintained his barn, house, and fences to keep everything in good repair. He paid attention to his animals to make sure they were in good health.

People commented about the beauty of his farm whenever they drove by. The white fences gleamed, the farmhouse looked like something off a postcard, and the fields were lush and green.

Travel down the road, though, and Ralph's farm got a different reaction. Ralph was lazy. He talked a lot about what he was going to do—but he never did anything. Most days, he just sat on his porch while neighboring farmers worked. His fence posts were

rotten and tottering. Weeds and fallen trees littered his property. The rails had collapsed off his porch and his house was covered in faded peeling paint. He wasted the gift that God and those before him had handed down to him, and as a result, his family struggled to put food on the table.

God loves hard work. Let's not be like Ralph. Let's determine that we'll be good stewards of all that God has given us, that we'll work hard at the tasks he gives us to do. That's especially important spiritually. Instead of leaving our children with memories of a life that was wasted, let's give our all when it comes to serving God. Let's leave them the example of a meticulously cared-for soul.

Lord, give me a good work ethic
and help me to do my best for you.

NOT WHAT SHE'D EXPECTED

Jesus Christ is the same yesterday and today and forever.
HEBREWS 13:8 NIV

This was *not* what Darlene had expected when she moved into her dream home in the country. It was a beautiful setting with woods on three sides and a lovely meadow and creek at the back of her acreage. She'd imagined peaceful mornings on the deck sipping a cup of tea and quiet afternoons outdoors reading a good book. But that's not what happened.

Her husband and their neighbor decided to go into farming now that they lived in the country. Her first clue that this was not going to be a good thing was when she saw where the guys had built the electric fence. It attached to her deck! Instead of the idyllic country living of her dreams, she now had several alarm clocks she didn't want.

She'd never forget that first springtime morning when the new rooster woke her at the crack of dawn, followed by the dinging of cow bells, baaing from the

sheep, and the clucking of chickens. Yes, all of them barely twenty feet from the back door of her dream house. And then there was the (ahem) fresh country air that wafted in her bedroom window. Definitely not what she'd expected.

Life often happens just like that. Everything's going well. We're living our dream life—and then out of nowhere, the unexpected happens or we get a wake-up call we didn't want. I'm so grateful that when those moments come to us, that they're never unexpected to God, and I'm thankful that in a world that's constantly changing, he *never* changes.

Father, thank you for always being the same. You are never caught off guard by my circumstances.

EXTENSIONS OF GOD'S HANDS

*Let each of you look out not only for his own interests,
but also for the interests of others.*
PHILIPPIANS 2:4 NKJV

The fall from the loft in the barn had left Roy with
a broken leg and injured back. The doctor said it would
be months before he could go back to work. After
Martha went to sleep each night, Roy fretted about
what they were going to do. Since they were just weeks
away from planting crops, the accident couldn't have
happened at a worse time.

Roy didn't know how his family would survive this
financial devastation, especially since they'd already been
struggling. If he couldn't get the seeds planted, there was
no hope for a harvest—but the doctor said he couldn't do
anything. Roy was too discouraged to even pray.

But two weeks after the accident, Roy was sitting on
the front porch when he noticed something unusual.
His usually quiet country lane was filled with cars and
trucks. Moments later, dozens of people walked across

his yard. As they got closer, he recognized members from his church, extended family, and farmers from all over the county.

One of them stepped up on the porch, "God told us to take care of you, Roy. We're here to plant your crops today, and we'll take turns coming to work throughout the summer until everything is harvested and taken to the market."

Roy's friends were practicing pure religion that day. They were extensions of God's hands of compassion as they cared for Roy's needs just as they would have done for their own. That's a beautiful example for all of us to follow. How could *you* carry the love of Jesus today to someone who needs a helping hand?

Lord, give me a heart of compassion for others.

THE INSURANCE PLAN

I know the plans I have for you, declares the LORD,
plans for welfare and not for evil,
to give you a future and a hope.
JEREMIAH 29:11 ESV

Like most farmers, Blake and Betty had gone through many up-and-down cycles financially. They'd been hit by a costly lawsuit from someone who'd been injured while visiting their farm. They'd had years when cattle sold at market for stellar prices, and others where they lost cattle from wild animal attacks, theft, and disease. They'd had the bumper crop years when they made lots of money, and then there were the ones where they'd pinched their pennies so hard that Lincoln squealed. Something had to change.

After praying about what to do, they set up an appointment with an agent who specialized in farm insurance. He talked to them about comprehensive liability insurance which would cover them if one of their animals got out in the road or someone got hurt on their property.

They discussed farmowner's insurance that would cover their property, their barns, and their tractors while they were driving them on the road. The policy would also provide coverage if their cattle were hit by lightning, attacked by wild dogs or other animals, or were stolen. Having the insurance plan would protect them from many of the situations that had blindsided them financially in the past.

From a spiritual standpoint, the best insurance policy we could ever have is serving Jesus. He covers us in all situations, and he has the perfect plan for us—one that will be for our good instead of harm. The great news is that he's already paid the cost, and because of him we can have hope and a future.

Lord, thank you for having the perfect plan for me.

SIMPLE TRUST

My God will supply all your needs
according to His riches in glory in Christ Jesus.
PHILIPPIANS 4:19 NASB

Bright and early every morning, Dan heads out
to feed the livestock on his farm. The chickens cluck,
pecking around his feet as he dumps out the bucket
of feed. The horses whinny and toss their heads in
excitement as they hear him shake the bucket of grain.
"Moos" greet him as he throws out hay for the cows.
The pigs oink in excitement as he dumps the bucket of
slop into their trough. None of them look shocked to
see him, because he does that every day.

Those farm animals don't have to worry about
where their next meal is coming from, because the
farmer takes care of them and provides what they need.
The same is true of us. God has promised to provide
our needs—and yet we worry and fret whenever things
get tight financially or we get in a tough situation. We
limit God by *our* abilities instead of focusing on his

unlimited capabilities. We look at the situations based on our lack of resources instead of looking at the vastness of his riches. We stress, forgetting about his perfect track record, failing to remember that the Bible doesn't record one story about the time God failed his children. Not one.

Just as those farm animals trust the farmer to bring their next meal, and they're standing there waiting on him when he gets there with their food, we can wait on him with complete trust that he will be all that we need for any situation.

Lord, thank you for always providing what I need. Whenever I allow worry to rule my mind, remind me that you're a faithful God with a proven track record.

WHAT'S THAT NOISE?

Be imitators of me, as I am of Christ.
1 CORINTHIANS 11:1 ESV

Lifting the last bag of groceries from the car, I heard a strange buzzing sound, almost like I had neglected to turn the car off, but I felt the key in my pocket. After walking into the house, I went from room to room looking for a noise. Nothing. I walked back outside to close the door and heard it again. Listening closely, I turned to look at the miniature red maple by the porch. It was filled with bees. Lots of buzzing bees. The swarm sounded much like a generator motor.

Bees swarm because the queen bee decides to leave the hive and seek out a place for a new one. When she leaves the original hive, she takes hundreds, if not thousands, of bees with her. They find a place to swarm while the scout bees go out and find a new hive location. The swarm could last for a few hours or longer.

Have you ever made a change in location and had hundreds of people move with you? Of course not. But

there are things you do every day that cause people to want to follow you.

It may be something as simple as picking up a piece of paper off the sidewalk in front of your church. Or it could be your leadership skills are better displayed through your attitude toward the homeless man on the side of the road.

Growing up, I often heard the phrase, "You may be the only Bible someone reads." In other words, people respect you as a leader and are watching what you do. Make sure that you are leading them in a good direction.

✳

Lord, help me be a good leader for others.

SCUPPIE TIME

The land yields its harvest;
God, our God, blesses us.
PSALM 67:6 NIV

"C'mon, y'all. Scuppie time!"

When you heard those words on the farm in the fall it could only mean one thing— the scuppernong grapes on the fence were ripe and ready for harvest. Time to make jelly!

For years, this had been a family activity. In fact, as my children were growing up, it was the only thing I ever heard anyone say specifically about returning home, "When I grow up, I'm coming back to the farm to make jelly."

The process of picking grapes (and eating a few along the way), boiling, squishing, juicing, and then making the jelly was fun. But I think the best part was that we all did it together. Not a lot of activities brought the entire family around the kitchen counter with one purpose. This tradition bonded us and drew us

closer together every year. And the tradition continued through the year as bow-trimmed jelly jars became our Christmas gift of choice.

When Jesus was young, his family likely did many things together. We don't know that they made jelly but we do know they went to the temple as a family. Joseph might have called the family to the carpenter shop to help with a project or to make something together.

Going to church is still a priority for many families. Other families make sure to gather around the table at least once a day for a meal. Hiking is a popular family pastime for others. Still others like to bake together. Does your family have something special that you do together on a regular basis?

Lord, remind me every day that I am an important part of your family. Show me ways I can draw closer to my brothers and sisters.

CHICKEN CONGENIALITY

Be devoted to one another in brotherly love;
give preference to one another in honor.
ROMANS 12:10 NASB

Any time I return home after being away, James comes running over to meet me with the same message, "Cock-a-doodle-do." Yes, James is a rooster.

Raising chickens is a popular trend. Farm fresh eggs are healthy and rich in nutrients. While the value of raising chickens for their eggs and meat is no surprise, you might not be expecting a chicken greeting every time you walk out your back door. Chickens are social, and in our barnyard, James is not the only one that frequently acknowledges a family member coming out into the yard.

Socialization is important in everyone's life. We all need friends. Perhaps the name of one person comes to mind when you hear the word friend. Friends make you feel loved, encourage you, and help you become a better person. You can call a real friend even at two in the morning.

But the best friend of all is Jesus. Some question how someone you can't visually connect with can be your friend, especially your best friend. Jesus can be your best friend because he is in your heart and that heart connection is the greatest kind of all. He is always with you and you can talk to him any time of the day or night. What a comfort to know he is there, and beyond that, he loves you more than any other friend could.

Hopefully you can echo the well-known song originally written as a poem by Joseph M. Scriven, "What a Friend We Have in Jesus."

Lord, what a treasure to have you as my best friend. Don't let me forget that the time I spend with you builds and strengthens our relationship.

WANDERING SHEEP

*You were like sheep going astray, but have now returned to
the Shepherd and Overseer of your souls.*

1 PETER 2:25 NKJV

Those sheep had been nothing but a nuisance since
Becky's husband, Cody, bought them from another
farmer and brought them home. Becky had lost count
of how many times she'd pulled into their driveway and
seen the sheep napping on their porch steps. Cody had
fixed the fence countless times, but those sheep had a
gift for getting out and wandering away.

Becky had completely lost patience with them the
week that Cody was out of town and three of the sheep
got loose. Becky chased them up one hill and down
another, across the street and through the meadow. Her
face was blood red—part of it from the hundred-degree
heat, and part of it from aggravation. It probably didn't
help matters any that Becky was six months pregnant.

The final straw came the day the sheep got out,
wandered into the yard of the new house down

the road, and ate thousands of dollars' worth of landscaping. The minute Cody got home, she met him at the door, hands on her hips and said, "Those sheep have to go."

Aren't you grateful that God didn't say those words about us? God refers to us as his sheep. Many of us are just like Cody's sheep—we strike out on our own and leave the security of where God placed us. We run from him when he chases us with love and we often mess up and leave destruction behind us. Life is always better when the Shepherd is in control. Do you need to return to his pasture today?

Father, help me to always return to you.

FROM CITY GIRL TO FARM GIRL

I will instruct you and teach you in the way you should go;
I will counsel you with my loving eye on you.
PSALM 32:8 NIV

Several years ago, we moved from the city to the farm. In previous years we had made many weekly trips to the family farm to take care of the garden and other things. The time finally came to sell the house in town and move to the country. We officially became fulltime farmers.

I wondered how this city girl was going to make the transition. For years I had prayed for God to make me willing to move since it was my husband's dream to live on the farm. But it took a while for me to get on board (the tractor, of course!). Once I knew it was time to move, I learned several things rather quickly.

The sound of crickets and tree frogs is a perfect lullaby. Waking up to the birds chirping, and yes, even the rooster crowing, starts the day off mindful of God's creation. Clean, country air feels really good to breathe (except when hay is being cut and it gets dusty).

Prayer time becomes very special when you can go outside and worship without city noises.

Home really is where the heart is.

Have you ever made a major change in your life? As hard as that can be, I hope you looked to God and learned many great lessons as you trusted him. When God directs you and you obediently follow, he will bless you in your new situation in ways you never imagined.

✳

Lord, moving is not easy. Give me confidence in every life change and bless me as I look to you for guidance.

JOHNNY APPLESEED

*I planted the seed, Apollos watered it,
but God has been making it grow.*
1 CORINTHIANS 3:6 NIV

In the early 1800's, John Chapman became known as "Johnny Appleseed." This prolific nurseryman traveled America's western frontier planting many acres of apple trees. Our vision quickly goes to hundreds of trees laden with the sweet, juicy apples we eat today. But according to Smithsonian.com, the apples from Johnny Appleseed's tree were bitter, not edible, and used to make hard apple cider.

What can we learn from this gentleman who loved the land? Some may concentrate on his widespread travel. Others look at his ability to grow apples that could be made into a strong drink. But the most significant thing Johnny Appleseed did was to carry around a pocket or bag full of apple seeds and spread them wherever he went. He knew that to grow quality plants they must be started from seed and spread widely.

As propagators of the Kingdom of God, we have an assignment similar to Johnny Appleseed's. We need to be spreading seeds wherever we go, seeds that will be watered from various places and eventually grow into strong believers. Our pocket full of seeds could include words, actions, gifts, and a lifestyle that lets others see God's love in everything we do.

When was the last time you sowed a seed with the potential to grow into a strong, healthy Christian? With your family? With your friends? With someone you sat down beside on a bus? Every day we come in contact with "soil" that is in desperate need of seeds. Don't hesitate to scatter them wildly.

Lord, may the seeds I plant grow into strong members of your family who will also begin to sow seeds of love. Give me a planting ground every day.

TENANT FARMERS

We are here for only a moment, visitors and strangers in the land as our ancestors were before us. Our days on earth are like a passing shadow, gone so soon without a trace.

1 CHRONICLES 29:15 NLT

Growing up on the farm, I learned about a lot of things I would have missed in the city. Just down the road (but still on the farm) lived a tenant family. They stayed on our land in exchange for working the land and helping to manage the farm.

As a little girl, I often went up to the tenant family's house to play with their children. The house was really small, but the children were plentiful and always ready to play jump rope or hopscotch. These were my friends and playmates. I learned an entirely different kind of life by watching and interacting with our tenant farmers.

Before too many years, the tenant farmer packed up his family and moved on. I didn't know where they went and I never saw them again.

We are actually on the same kind of journey. We are living on land that really doesn't belong to us. We

may hold the deed to the property, but we are just passing through this world on our way to a much better destination. We are working for the Master of the land for his benefit. We even get to play with his other children while we are here.

God has entrusted his beautiful world to us. Let's double our efforts and be the best tenant farmers we can be. Let's take time to enjoy the land he's given us. Let's praise God and give him the glory for the creation that he allows us to enjoy.

Lord, thank you for your provision
of a beautiful world to live in.

JEFF'S BIRTHDAY PARTY

*"Come, follow me... and I will send you out
to fish for people."*
MATTHEW 4:19 NIV

Jeff's tenth birthday was a week away. "I want to have a fishing party at Grandpa's farm."

A fishing party? We agreed as long as certain rules were followed. When we arrived at the farm with ten young men and a few teenagers to help bait hooks, the boys eagerly jumped out of the car and ran down the bank to the pond. They spread out along the edge of the water and began to fish.

About three minutes into the party, Ben began to yell. "Whoa! I got one. Somebody help me! I need to get him on the bank. This has got to be a big fish."

And it was. A beautiful five-pound bass. "I'm going to mount this one," Ben said.

"Okay, boys," Grandpa said, "let's get back to fishing."

The boys baited their hooks. But instead of spreading out around the bank, they looked to see

where Ben was fishing. One by one each boy moved over to join him. Ben moved over a bit. The entire crowd moved with him. It was like a little cluster of fishermen moving as one entity.

Ben had something the boys wanted: Fisherman's luck. They wanted to be just like him.

Have you ever had anyone want to be just like you? When you move from place to place do others follow hoping to have what you have? That is exactly what we want to happen with our faith. We want others to migrate to where we are, hoping to catch what we have—a faith based on our desire to be just like Jesus.

✳

Lord, help me to be a good fisherman for you.

THE FARMER IN THE DELL

"The harvest is plentiful but the workers are few."
MATTHEW 9:37 NIV

One of the first musical games most children learn is "The Farmer in the Dell." The farmer starts out in the middle, and as the song and play continues, he chooses others to be part of his family. Those chosen join him in the middle and become part of the farm family.

This has always been looked upon as a fun song for children to play during recess at school or some other time. But the reality is that it does take a lot of people to run a farm, and farmers often have to call on family and friends to get the work done. When it's time for harvest or hay baling, it must be done quickly before the weather ruins the crops.

This is not unlike God's Kingdom. There is so much to be done and it is time sensitive. Jesus is coming back and we don't know when. So until then the workers must be about the business of telling people about him, about harvesting people for God's purpose here on earth. We

are God's hands and feet and we need to not grow weary. Time is short so we must keep working.

Do you know people who are searching? Are there people in your circle of influence who need to know that there is eternal life just waiting for them? Why not accelerate your efforts to spread God's love? In fact, take a lesson from "The Farmer in the Dell" and enlist others to help you.

Lord, help me to take my job of being your worker seriously. Bless my efforts to tell others about you.

GOLF BALLS OR EGGS

Let us consider how we may spur one another on toward love and good deeds.
HEBREWS 10:24 NIV

The chickens had not started laying. All the books said we should have our first eggs between four and seven months, and Farmer John was getting worried.

"When should my chickens start laying eggs?" he asked a neighbor farmer. "I think we should be having some eggs soon."

"Well," Sal said, "I had a similar problem."

"Oh, what did you do?"

"My wife had some decorative wooden eggs. We put them in the nest to see if maybe the power of suggestion would work."

"Did it?"

"Sure did. The very next morning there were eggs in the nest."

Farmer John took that advice. When he got home he looked to see if he could find any fake eggs.

Not having much luck, he asked his daughter if she happened to have any fake eggs.

"No," she said, "but my hubby has some golf balls."

"Well, I might as well give them a try. I don't have anything to lose."

Farmer John went home and filled the laying box with golf balls. The next morning he went to feed the chickens, and guess what he found? All the golf balls were pushed to the side and three eggs replaced them.

Sometimes we are just like those chickens— stubborn. God tries to get us to move in a certain direction and we won't do it. During those times he has to nudge us in some way to get us to do what he wants us to accomplish. Are there any areas of your life where God needs to put a golf ball today?

Lord, make me sensitive to your nudges and help me listen to your voice for direction.

GROWING WEEDS

Create in me a pure heart, O God,
and renew a steadfast spirit within me.
PSALM 51:10 NIV

All summer I see my farmer husband out in the garden pulling weeds. No matter what the weather, he is there. "You can't let them get ahead of you," he says, "or you will never catch up."

I agree with my farmer. Weeds can come up overnight or double in size at the blink of an eye. The longer you leave the weed in the ground, the more difficult it is to pull it. As they grow, weeds get more firmly anchored and you have to pull harder to make them let go of the soil.

Sin is kind of like those weeds. It sneaks up on us at the most unexpected times. And once it takes hold, it becomes harder and harder to get rid of as time goes by.

George learned the hard way. He once took a pack of gum from the store to see if he could get away with it. After a time of stealing small items, George began to

take larger items. He knew it was risky, but the thrill of getting things he couldn't afford overrode his knowledge of right and wrong. George spent time in prison.

While George was incarcerated, he came to know the Lord and realized how wrong he had been. He had let weeds grow in his life. Because he didn't pull them out, they became stronger.

Once he met Jesus, George knew there was a better way to live. He decided to spend his life telling others to get rid of the weeds while they were small. Do you have any weeds that need to be pulled from *your* life?

Lord, show me the weeds in my life while they are small.

TOMATO SUCKERS

Like newborn babies, crave pure spiritual milk,
so that by it you may grow up in your salvation.
1 PETER 2:2 NIV

There is nothing like a home-grown tomato. One
of summer's best offerings is soft white bread with a
generous helping of mayonnaise, salt and pepper, and a
bright red, right-from-the vine tomato.

If you buy your tomatoes from the corner produce
stand, you may not know what it takes to produce that
amazing red fruit. As the tomato vines grow, their vines
not only have the yellow flowers that will turn into the
fruit, small off-shoots appear at various points along the
vine. These are called "suckers." They make the plants
look good and full. But the farmer knows that to grow
the best tomatoes, he will have to walk the garden and
pinch off the suckers. Otherwise, they will sap valuable
energy from the growing tomatoes.

The same thing can happen to us if we're not
careful. There are things in our lives that become

suckers. At first they may appear to be a healthy growing part of our lives, but then we realize that they are taking strength that we needed for other things like family, friends, and work.

God has given us discernment to figure out what the good things are in our lives and what the things are that demand our time, attention, and money and yet have little value. If we can eliminate those suckers, we will have more energy to put into the things that matter. Then we'll be able to produce fruit for the Kingdom.

Is there a sucker in your life that needs to be pinched off so that you can better serve God?

✳

Lord, show me what suckers need
to be eliminated from my life.

TRAPPED

God is faithful; he will not let you be tempted beyond what you can bear. But when you are tempted, he will also provide a way out.

1 CORINTHIANS 10:13 NIV

I felt like I was in the middle of a horror movie. Our windows were covered in black. Angry black that moved and buzzed as loud as a chain saw. Thousands of honey bees had swarmed, trapping me inside my house. What would I do if they made their way indoors?

Thankfully, I didn't have to answer that question that day. But you can imagine my shock on another day when I opened the door to our bedroom and hundreds of honey bees flew in my direction. I slammed the door, and quickly stuffed towels at the bottom so none could escape. I wanted those bees to stay trapped in that room. My husband didn't have to ask if something was wrong when I called for him. The panic in my voice said it all.

The bees had gotten in through a small hole in the outside wall. No telling how long they'd been there

because we had honey dripping between the studs. That was an awful experience to be trapped by those bees. It took someone who knew what they were doing to get us out of that predicament.

We often go through something similar in our lives—trapped by circumstances like financial difficulties, health problems, and broken relationships—and often we see no way out. But that's where our faithful God says he won't give us more than we can bear. He knows what he's doing and he will come to us and remove whatever has stung our lives and trapped us. He will make a way of escape.

Lord, thank you for always rescuing me.

FARM SANCTUARY

"Seek first his kingdom and his righteousness, and all these things will be given to you as well."
MATTHEW 6:33 NIV

Owen lived in the local boys' home. He had never been to a working farm. However, one of the house parents had to visit a friend in the country and took Owen with him.

Farmer Bill was glad to see Owen. "Would you like to ride around the farm and see it?"

"Sure," Owen replied.

The two got in Bill's utility vehicle and went through the pasture and into the woods. Bill explained every fence, animal, and salt block to Owen and shared about its purpose. When they got to the river, they came to a little clearing. There were flowers planted, a cement stool, a sign with a Bible verse on it, and all you could hear was the soothing sound of water running downstream.

"What's this?" Owen asked.

"This is my personal sanctuary. I come here when I have something on my mind. I sit on that stool and have a conversation with God. Would you like to try it?"

Owen nodded. Bill watched him get out and walk over to the stool. He sat facing the water for over five minutes.

Owen stood and rejoined Bill. "Feel better?" Bill asked.

"You know I think I do." Owen smiled—the first one Bill had seen.

Everyone needs a place to go and meet with God. It may be by the river, in the field, or on a porch overlooking the farm. It could be your favorite armchair. The place doesn't really matter. The important thing is that you find that personal sanctuary where it is just you and God.

Do you visit your sanctuary often? You should.

Lord, thank you for our precious times together.

FARM FREEDOM

It is for freedom that Christ has set us free. Stand firm, then, and do not let yourselves be burdened again by a yoke of slavery.

GALATIANS 5:1 NIV

Very few people grow up without in some way being touched by the stories of *Little House on the Prairie*. The television series continues to run daily and entertain families of all ages.

At one point in the series, Charles Ingalls said to his young son, "You'll be free and independent, son, on a farm."

For sure there is a special freedom in getting up every morning when the rooster crows, drinking your coffee as dawn breaks, having a quiet time while watching the world wake up, then putting on your overalls to go to work. With the farm as their workplace, most farmers would agree with Ingalls. There is a freedom and independence you find in few other places.

But don't you think freedom and independence is something that every person desires? The good news

is that you don't have to be a farmer to have that. God has made total freedom and independence available to every person. All you have to do is accept his Son Jesus and live according to his plan for you.

Some people have resisted making that decision because it feels restrictive, like they have to give up something more than they are receiving. But that is the opposite of what happens. When you give up your selfish desires and began to seek God's choices in your life, you will discover a freedom and independence you never knew existed.

Want real freedom and independence? Open your heart to God's love and ask him to fill you with his freedom.

Lord, thank you that I am truly free in you.

SECURITY IN THE LAND

Those who work their land will have abundant food.
PROVERBS 12:11 NIV

President George W. Bush once said, "We're a blessed nation because we can grow our own food. A nation that can feed its people is a nation more secure."

A farmer at heart, President Bush realized the importance of the land and its bounty. Our country is able to use the land to grow healthy foods that will keep us strong. And in that, we can find security.

But even having enough food is not real security. When you mention feeling secure, there is only one way to feel that—through knowing God and resting in him.

Mary's husband, William, had been sick for some time. Caring for him brought much extra responsibility and physical work. Many people said to Mary, "How do you do this 24/7? Don't you worry about getting it all done, or paying the bills, or how you are going to take care of the farm?"

Mary's answer was always the same. "No, I don't worry. I just trust God. He has never failed to provide what we needed. I have all the security I need. I am confident he will take care of me. We have never been without food or help so far and I know that will not change."

Do you have that kind of security in your life? Do you know without a shadow of a doubt that God will take care of you? He will.

Perhaps you know someone like Mary who could use a hand in some way. Why not step out today and be part of someone else's security? God loves to use his people to touch others.

Lord, you have given us land to grow food. Thank you that we have good, fresh things to eat.

WHAT'S YOUR ENVIRONMENT?

*"It had been planted in good soil by abundant water
so that it would produce branches, bear fruit
and become a splendid vine."*

EZEKIEL 17:8 NIV

Virginia and Chris are new aquaponic farmers. "We have enjoyed working together in our garden and decided to try a new way of growing things," Virginia said. "It's been educational and we look forward to our first harvest."

Aquaponic gardening has similarities to regular farming. But some things are new and different. For example, when planting in regular soil, many farmers broadcast the seed and plan to thin plants later. They pay no attention to the way or where the seeds land. The soil is loose, so as the roots seek the soil and the shoots seek the sunlight, the plants will position themselves in the proper way to grow.

Aquaponic gardening is different. A tightly packed growing medium makes it more difficult for the plants to grow properly unless the seeds are placed in exactly

the right position. If planted haphazardly the new aquaponic plants could grow upside down—roots on top and shoots in the water. The soil has a tremendous effect on the success and production of the plants.

Aren't we like those plants? If we are in an environment where we can thrive, we grow, produce fruit, and are successful. If we find ourselves topsy-turvy in a place where we cannot move or it's difficult to correct ourselves, we are doomed for failure.

God has created an environment in which we can thrive, but he also allows us to make choices. We can control our environments by our choices in friends, work, and the places we go. What's your current environment? Make sure it provides the spiritual soil and nutrients you need to grow strong.

❊

Lord, help me make good choices.

ARE YOU A FOLLOWER?

*They pulled their boats up on shore,
left everything and followed him.*
LUKE 5:11 NIV

Douglas opened the back door and stepped onto the porch. The chickens were already at the front corner of the chicken yard poised to see who was coming out.

Any time the back door opens all the chickens quickly move to meet you. They don't even know yet if you are bringing a treat but they are ready to see their human peeps. Chickens may not be known for their hearing, but it is almost impossible for Douglas to sneak out the back door.

When you get to the chicken yard, the excitement continues. When you go to the food box to get the food, they move over there. When you get the hose to give them clean water, they meet you at the water bucket. If you reach for worms as a treat, they really get excited. Douglas could probably circle the fence and the chickens would gladly do the same.

People are followers, too. We tend to gravitate toward people we want to emulate. Are you following the right people?

Your first choice of who to follow should, of course, be Jesus. But it is easy to be enticed astray when your motive is to fit into the crowd or make people like you.

Make the decision now to follow him in all you do. You don't even have to worry about whether he likes you or not. He loves you no matter what. After all, he died for you. There could be no greater love!

Father, help me to pick friends who will follow you.

FEEDING TIME

*Do your best to present yourself to God as one approved,
a worker who does not need to be ashamed and who
correctly handles the word of truth.*

2 TIMOTHY 2:15 NIV

The farm driveway is beautiful in the springtime.
Both sides are filled with gorgeous bulbs—daffodils
and lily-of-the-valley—some planted decades ago. It
seems a little odd that you feed daffodils, lily of the
valley, and other bulbs after they have bloomed and
are dying. But as they rest during the cold hard winter
they are preparing to come back the next year stronger,
healthier, and bigger. There's definitely a benefit to that
method of feeding. Even though we seem to be feeding
them at the wrong time, it's the right time for those
bulbs to store food and get ready for the next blooming.

We're somewhat like those bulbs. We feed on the
Word of God. We may not be in a time of great need, but
it is important to keep feeding. When we consistently
study the Bible, we are preparing ourselves to bloom.

Or we could be preparing for a time of need when we aren't able to study as much. Learning and memorizing God's Word throughout the year will prepare us to stand strong and to bloom in the hard times.

Sheryl was in the hospital. She had been sick for several weeks and still was not feeling well enough to read or have company. She says, "I don't feel like doing much but as I lay here, Scripture from my quiet times comes to mind and gives me peace. I even remember stories of God's faithfulness from Sunday School."

Are you storing up God's Word for those hard times?

Lord, help me to share the wisdom you've given me with others.

WHAT ARE YOU LEAVING BEHIND?

Thanks be to God, who always leads us as captives in Christ's triumphal procession and uses us to spread the aroma of the knowledge of him everywhere.
2 CORINTHIANS 2:14 NIV

Our farm land includes the site of a Revolutionary War rifle factory. We have plowed, and built, and used the land for other things, and in the process, we've found small remnants of the rifle business. Occasionally we find pieces of plows and other farm implements. One of the treasures is an old anvil found in an abandoned barn. The things that are left behind give us clues to the people who came before us.

I've often thought about the legacy I am leaving for my children. What will they think of the things they find? What will my possessions tell them about my life? Am I leaving them something more important than things? Am I instilling faith in them now that will last forever?

My mother's legacy is not in the things she left me, although I treasure them as visual reminders of her

love. The things that matter most are that she loved me and encouraged me from the time I was born until she died. She showed me how to love people and to give generously of what she had. Mother loved the Lord and she enjoyed giving her testimony to others.

My prayer is that when I'm gone, my children, grandchildren, and great-grandchildren will continue to feel the love I have for them, and that the sweet fragrance of my love for Jesus will remain.

What about you? What do you want to leave behind for your family?

Lord, may I spread the sweet aroma of your love everywhere I go and may it linger long after I am gone.

ARE YOU WATCHING THE GRASS GROW?

I lift up my eyes to the mountains—
where does my help come from?
My help comes from the LORD,
the Maker of heaven and earth.

PSALM 121:1-2 NIV

Sunday afternoon visits to my dad's farm were always special. Driving down the long driveway that circled the pond was the signal for city thoughts to flee and a new calm spirit to emerge for a few hours. The children were so eager they wanted to jump from the car as soon as it slowed down. Once we stopped, got out, and walked over to the porch where Dad was sitting, his first words almost always were, "Welcome. Come on over here and have a seat and watch the grass grow."

Now for a type A, gotta-be-doing-something-every-minute girl, sitting around and watching the grass grow didn't seem like a productive or fun idea. But everyone sat down and prepared to enjoy our time away from the city hustle and bustle.

Several interesting things happened when we had those Sunday afternoon grass-growing sessions. Dad began to share stories with us. We lovingly called them "lectures" because we always learned something, usually something that strengthened our faith.

By waiting to see the grass grow (which we never did), we observed the beauty around us in God's creation. We learned that sitting on the porch with family is never wasted time. It's a treasure as bonds are strengthened. And we learned that hummingbirds, bees, and other free spirited things will welcome you to "their" porch if you sit long enough.

All of the above was in its own way a worship experience. What out-of-the-ordinary ways has God shown himself to you lately?

※

Lord, thank you for family time that includes lessons of your faithfulness and beauty.

WHAT'S YOUR ROADBLOCK?

*Watch out for those who cause divisions and
put obstacles in your way that are contrary to the teaching
you have learned. Keep away from them.*

ROMANS 16:17 NIV

After every storm, Bud has to ride the trail checking
for trees down and any damage on the farm. With thick
woods on the property, he's never sure what he will find.

The last storm was a doozy and when Bud started
out he saw limbs and sticks down everywhere. He
stopped to move a few limbs and continued down to
the creek. Everything looked okay. But once he crossed
the creek, he could only go a few feet until a big tree was
across the road.

Up until this point it had been fairly simple to pick
up the limbs that were in the way. But this tree was
going to take the chain saw, a lot of work, and probably
some helpers.

That's exactly what happens to us as we travel our
life's journey. We are going along just fine. We may have

to move a few small limbs or sticks but overall nothing major. Then all of a sudden we come upon a big tree or other obstacle in our path. It may seem insurmountable, but with a lot of hard work and some help, we can clear it out of the way.

Another important factor to overcoming big, fat trees in our lives is prayer. While we are working and making changes to get rid of the obstacle, let's remember to lift our situation up in prayer, asking God to show us the best way to overcome it. He will surely do that.

*Lord, clearly show me your path
to overcoming life's obstacles.*

CAUGHT IN THE BRIERS

The fear of the Lord is a fountain of life,
turning a person from the snares of death.
PROVERBS 14:27 NIV

Gold Dust was the best horse ever. He was a Tennessee Walker, and riding Gold Dust was a smooth and easy ride. He usually stayed right around the barn though the pasture covered many acres.

On one occasion, Gold Dust was nowhere in sight. Ray realized he hadn't seen the horse that morning and became concerned. Because Gold Dust was faithful to stay near the barn, Ray decided to look for him. He drove through the pasture and found no sign of him. Then he went down by the creek. The horses rarely went that far, but Ray decided he'd better check every possible corner.

As Ray traveled down the bank to the creek, he heard the water running over the rocks. Listening more carefully, he thought he heard the soft whinny of a horse. Sure enough, there stood Gold Dust tangled up in briers and barbed wire.

Ray quickly freed the horse and led him to the creek to drink. Gold Dust drank for a long time as he rehydrated his body. Patting him on the flank, Ray said, "I sure am glad I found you. You really needed some water, didn't you, fella?"

We are sometimes surprised by the things of the world. They look enticing but turn out to be briers that ensnare us and hold us back from the good things our bodies need. The snares of the world could be friends, hobbies, work, or many other things that keep us from drinking from you. When you find yourself getting thirsty, run to the Source.

※

Lord, help me to always stand strong in you.
Keep me from the things that would ensnare me.

GREAT HUNTING

"Go therefore and make disciples of all nations, baptizing them in the name of the Father and of the Son and of the Holy Spirit, teaching them to observe all that I have commanded you. And behold, I am with you always, to the end of the age."

MATTHEW 28:19-20 ESV

There's a part of the farm that has always been kept for hunting. That's where the dove field, deer blind, and other hunting areas are, and Farmer Stu works hard to keep the fields ready for the hunters. Families often come to hunt together.

Josh and Martin are brothers and they always hunt together. When turkey season opens, they are usually the first to call Stu and ask if the fields are ready.

"Of course," Stu always replies. "Come on over."

Josh and Martin hunt in different places, so they don't really know what the other has gotten until they get back together.

On this occasion Josh was carrying two turkeys.

"Awesome," Martin said. "I didn't hear your shots."

"That's because I killed both these turkeys with one shot!"

"I've never known anyone to do that."

As believers we may not kill turkeys. But we do hunt for seekers and others who need to hear the gospel. Often once we begin talking about faith and the difference it makes in our lives, we find more than one person within earshot who is interested in hearing the gospel. At that moment, we realize we are on a hunt on God's behalf, looking to bring others into a relationship of faith in him.

Don't worry about getting two new believers with every share. Numbers aren't important. The important thing is that everyone has a chance to hear.

Happy hunting!

Lord, help me to be mindful that there are people who need to hear about your love.

REFLECTIONS IN THE POND

We all, with unveiled face, beholding the glory of the Lord, are being transformed into the same image from one degree of glory to another. For this comes from the Lord who is the Spirit.

2 CORINTHIANS 3:18 ESV

Sunrises are always beautiful. But I don't think many are as gorgeous as the sun coming up over the farm pond. I sat in my favorite chair watching the pinkish orange glow rise over the trees. It didn't take long for the world to come alive. Part of the beauty of early morning is that the sun is at just the right angle for the pond to reflect the landscape around it. You can look at the trees, the barn, and any flowers in bloom, and then look in the pond to see a perfect mirror likeness.

During my quiet time, God reminded me that he wants me to do the same thing that pond is doing. He wants me to reflect his likeness to everyone I encounter.

The pool is full of water and therefore it is able to reflect the things around it. How could I possibly reflect

anything? If I stay close to God by reading his Word and talking to him often, I will be ready to reflect his love in all ways. If I am full of the Living Water—Jesus—I will be able to reflect God's image to a world that desperately needs him. And when others see the image of God in my life, I will be able to share the story of his love for them.

✳

Father, I want to reflect you to others.
Fill me with your Living Water so I will show a clear,
perfect picture of your love.

OLD MCDONALD'S FARM

Just as each of us has one body with many members, and these members do not all have the same function, so in Christ we, though many, form one body, and each member belongs to all the others.

ROMANS 12:4-5 NIV

It always brings a smile to those around us when they hear a child sing "Old McDonald Had a Farm." Most children in America probably learned their animal sounds from singing about Old McDonald's animals.

One thing we know from Old McDonald. His farm was diverse. I'm not sure what the original lyrics included, but over the years many animals were added. Some were exotic, some foreign, and some probably fabricated. But there always seemed to be room for all.

These days it's not so much that way. Most farmers specialize. Whether growing varied crops, raising cattle, sheep, goats, or running a dairy, the everyday chores are much easier when concentrated in one area.

Many of us have probably had to learn the lesson

that Old McDonald did—it's easier to become an expert about one thing than to try to know everything about everything.

Often that's true in life. If you can specialize and become really good in one area, you are stronger and have more to offer others, and that's kind of the way God designed it.

We are all part of the body of Christ. But the key word is part. That means we can't do everything—we have to be responsible for *our* part—so we need to learn all we can and become experts in the role that we fill.

What part are you? Don't you want to be the best member of the body of Christ you can possibly be?

Lord, help me to fulfill your purpose for me.

PECAN HARVEST

From the fruit of their mouth a person's stomach is filled;
with the harvest of their lips they are satisfied.
PROVERBS 18:20 NIV

Like everything else on the farm, pecan harvest is
a job that can't wait. If you hold off too long and the
pecans sit out in the weather, they will rot. If you don't
hurry, birds and squirrels will think you left the meaty
nuts for them.

One Sunday afternoon, Chuck decided it was
time to collect pecans from the trees lining the farm
driveway. After lunch he called his grandchildren ages
ten, eight, and five over, "I will pay you a dollar for every
bucket of pecans picked up." Chuck gave them buckets
and showed them how to choose the good nuts and
leave rotten and half-eaten ones on the ground.

The adults visited in the house while doing the
lunch dishes. Auntie walked over to the window. "Hey,
y'all. Come look at this."

Abigail, the five-year-old, had enlisted her four-year-old and two-year-old cousins as well as her uncle. She had "hired" them to help her pick up pecans with the promise of a popsicle when they were done. Not surprisingly, Abigail got more pecans than anyone else that day.

Sometimes we can't do it all ourselves. We have to enlist help.

God planned the expansion of his Kingdom that way. He didn't intend for just the twelve disciples to tell people about Jesus. He didn't mean for only those who met Jesus personally to tell others about him. God intended for all believers to tell others about him and encourage their brothers and sisters to do the same.

What about you? Are you doing your part or could you enlist a few friends to help you?

❋

Lord, give me enthusiasm for your work.

HUMMINGBIRD FRIENDS

"Where could we get enough bread in this remote place to feed such a crowd?"

MATTHEW 15:33 NIV

Hummingbirds are often thought of as unfriendly or skittish. They swarm around the feeder until a human decides to come out. Then they flee. Not so at the Carpenters' house.

Tim Carpenter had lived on the hill at the farm for years. Every year one of his early spring priorities was to get the hummingbird feeders filled and hung on the porch. He had six feeders, and most of them had to be filled every day.

The hummingbirds got used to Tim sitting on the porch watching them as they buzzed to get nourishment so they could keep flying around. Some days he counted over a hundred little red and tan birds jockeying for a spot at one of the feeders. Tim finally got to where he could hold the feeder in his hand and the birds would come close to him to eat.

Have you ever thought of yourself as anything like a hummingbird? Do you cluster with other believers wanting to get your nourishment from God but when a nonbeliever comes near, you flee as if you have nothing to offer? Eventually you become closer to him and are compelled to let others know the Good News you have discovered.

God is our source of nourishment. Unless we get closer to him, we do not have the boldness to step out in his name and bring in others. Next time you see a hummingbird, ask God to show you those you need to reach to come feed on his Word. Then act on his direction. He wants to use you to feed others.

Lord, thank you for your constant nourishment for me.

LOST?

*In all your ways submit to him,
and he will make your paths straight.*

PROVERBS 3:6 NIV

Farmer Grady loved his farm. He knew every inch of the four hundred acres. To the casual visitor, it seemed like a good place to get lost. But to Grady it was an extension of the life he knew so well.

On one of her visits to the farm, Grady's daughter, Elyse, asked if she could ride around the farm. "Do you think I can find my way?" she asked her dad.

"Of course. I made a map and there's a copy on the dash of the vehicle. If you have any problems, just call me."

Elyse set out to enjoy the land and to hopefully see a few animals. She came to a spot, however, where she had to choose to go to the right or to take the sharp left. The map wasn't helpful, so she called her dad. "I think I'm lost. Can you help?"

"Sure. Do you see a tree?"

"Dad, there are thousands of trees on your property."

"Yes, but do you see one that is bent to the left beside a tall pine near the triangle?"

"Oh, yeah."

"Turn there and you will soon see the barn."

Sure enough Elyse soon found the barn. Her father knew exactly where she was all along.

Have you ever felt lost? We may not know where we are, but God always does. Even if we don't know our way around the world we live in, we have only to ask and God will give us directions to find our way.

Isn't that comforting that he knows where we are and that he can tell us how to get back on the straight path if we'll just ask him?

Lord, keep me on the straight path.

to: _____

from: _____

PRAY LIKE This

A 52-WEEK PRAYER JOURNAL

Illustration & Design

Kristi Smith
Juicebox Designs, Nashville, Tennessee

Editorial Team

Michael Kelley
Content Development

Susan Hill
Content Editor

Jon Rodda
Art Director

Joel Polk
Editorial Team Leader

Brian Daniel
Manager, Short-Term

Brandon Hiltibidal
Director, Discipleship and Groups Ministry

© 2020 LifeWay Press®

No part of this book may be reproduced or transmitted in any form or by any means, electronic or mechanical, including photocopying and recording, or by any information storage or retrieval system, except as may be expressly permitted in writing by the publisher. Requests for permission should be addressed in writing to LifeWay Press®; One LifeWay Plaza; Nashville, TN 37234.

ISBN 978-1-0877-1680-0 • Item 005826967
Dewey Decimal 242.5

Subject headings:
PRAYER/DEVOTIONAL LITERATURE/LORD'S PRAYER

Unless otherwise noted, all Scripture quotations are taken from the Christian Standard Bible®, Copyright © 2017 by Holman Bible Publishers. Used by permission. Christian Standard Bible® and CSB® are federally registered trademarks of Holman Bible Publishers.

To order additional copies of this resource, write to LifeWay Resources Customer Service; One LifeWay Plaza; Nashville, TN 37234; fax 615-251-5933; call toll free 800-458-2772; order online at LifeWay.com; or email orderentry@lifeway.com. Printed in the United States of America

Groups Ministry Publishing
LifeWay Resources • One LifeWay Plaza • Nashville, TN 37234

Printed in China

TABLE OF CONTENTS

HOW TO USE THIS DEVOTIONAL

This journal provides a 52-week guided experience for individuals to explore the Lord's Prayer and apply it to their prayer lives. Each week is divided into five days of personal study with journal space to record what you learn. As you study each assigned Scripture reading, you'll be prompted by the following questions:

- What does this passage teach me about God?

- How does it instruct my prayer life?

- Am I obeying this Scripture?

- If not, what changes do I need to make?

Use the space provided to record your thoughts and reflections. It's also a good idea to write down your prayer requests and then go back and record how God responded to your prayer requests, what you are learning, and new insights you've gained from your Bible reading.

INTRODUCTION

Jesus was a prayer warrior. Although He was the Son of God, He recognized the necessity of constantly abiding in a relationship of dependency on His Father. His disciples, noticing Jesus' habit of seeking time alone with the Father, requested, "Lord, teach us to pray, just as John also taught his disciples" (Luke 11:1). Jesus' response, as recorded by Matthew, was both simple and profound, both practical and deeply spiritual:

Our Father in heaven,

your name be honored as holy.

Your kingdom come.

Your will be done

on earth as it is in heaven.

Give us today our daily bread.

And forgive us our debts,

as we also have forgiven our debtors.

And do not bring us into temptation,

but deliver us from the evil one.

Matthew 6:9-13

The Lord's Prayer, as it's known today, is one of the most familiar passages in Scripture. Yet far too many Christians, caught up in the rush of daily life, don't make time to pray. In failing to follow Jesus' example, they're neglecting a discipline that's absolutely critical to an intimate, growing relationship with God.

Pray Like This takes a fresh look at each phrase in the Lord's Prayer to reveal its meaning and its implications for our prayer lives and our daily lives. We'll understand the significance of calling on God as Father, honoring His holy name, seeking His kingdom and His will, acknowledging our dependence on Him for every daily need, forgiving other people as He has forgiven us, and relying on His protection and deliverance from evil.

Following Jesus' Lord's Prayer will lead us to fall more in love with our heavenly Father and grow in our desire to engage in conversation with Him. As we study and apply Jesus' words, may we develop a more vibrant prayer life that leads to worship, spiritual maturity, dependence on God, and a knowledge of His will.

OUR FATHER IN HEAVEN,
YOUR NAME BE HONORED AS HOLY.
YOUR KINGDOM COME.
YOUR WILL BE DONE
ON EARTH AS IT IS IN HEAVEN.
GIVE US TODAY OUR DAILY BREAD.

AND FORGIVE US OUR DEBTS,
AS WE ALSO HAVE
FORGIVEN OUR DEBTORS.

AND DO NOT BRING US
INTO TEMPTATION,
BUT DELIVER US
FROM THE EVIL ONE.

MATTHEW 6: 9-13 CSB

Section One

LORD, TEACH US TO PRAY

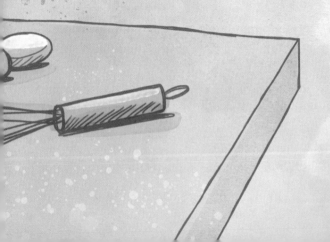

WHY PRAY?

As Christians, most of us know we should pray, but how often do we ponder the question, "Why pray?" If we view prayer as simply something we should do, we will never experience the vibrant prayer life God intends for us to enjoy. But if we are mindful of why we pray, we'll have good reason to devote ourselves to prayer. God created us to have a relationship with Him. Prayer—along with Scripture reading—are two of the primary ways we come to know God and experience Him in day-to-day life. As our prayer life develops and matures, our intimacy with God increases. There's a dramatic difference between simply knowing about God and knowing God. In our relationships with other people, we grow closer as we spend time together and communicate with one another. It's impossible to know someone well if we don't invest time in the relationship.

The same is true of our relationship with God. Prayer is our opportunity to communicate with our Creator. We have the privilege of telling Him what's on our heart, asking for His provision, confessing our sins, giving thanks, and offering praise and worship. It's through the process of prayer that God aligns our will with His, imparts His strength, and guides our daily life. As you read the assigned Scriptures this week, ask yourself: What does this passage teach me about God? How does it instruct my prayer life? Am I obeying this Scripture? If not, what changes do I need to make? Journal your answers and reflections.

DAY 1
PHILIPPIANS 4:6-7

_____

_____

_____

_____

_____

_____

_____

_____

_____

_____

DAY 3
PSALM 142:1-5

_____

_____

_____

_____

_____

_____

_____

_____

_____

_____

DAY 4
ROMANS 12:12

DAY 5
EPHESIANS 6:18

WEEK 2
THE POSSIBILITY OF PRAYER

Prayer is a subject that is or should be close to the core of every Christian's walk with God. Despite that, many of us live with a sense of longing when we think about our prayer lives. We know we should pray, we might even desire to pray with greater fervency, yet we aren't growing in our capacity for joy in prayer. But the Bible clearly teaches that God intends for His children to enjoy a vibrant prayer life.

Perhaps part of our struggle is we don't always know how to pray. If that's the case, we find ourselves in good company because Jesus' disciples felt the same way. When Jesus' closest followers asked Him to teach them to pray, He answered with what we know as the Lord's Prayer, a text that still instructs

Christ followers today in the discipline of talking and listening to God (Matt. 6:9-13). In the coming weeks, we'll take a close look at the Lord's Prayer. As we prepare to study the Lord's Prayer, we'll spend time this week examining Scriptures that show us what is possible in the life of someone who is devoted to prayer. God has called His people to prayer and He works mightily through our petitions. As you read the assigned Scriptures this week, ask yourself: What does this passage teach me about God? How does it instruct my prayer life? Am I obeying this Scripture? If not, what changes do I need to make? Journal your answers and reflections.

DAY 1
PSALM 34:4-6

_____
_____
_____
_____
_____
_____
_____
_____
_____

DAY 3
1 JOHN 5:14-15

_____
_____
_____
_____
_____
_____
_____
_____
_____

DAY 4
DANIEL 10:12

_____
_____
_____
_____
_____
_____
_____
_____
_____
_____

DAY 5
JAMES 5:13-15

_____
_____
_____
_____
_____
_____
_____
_____
_____
_____

Section Two
THE FATHERHOOD OF GOD

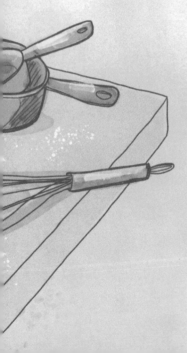

OUR FATHER IN HEAVEN
AN INTIMATE TITLE FOR GOD

When Jesus' disciples asked Him to teach them to pray, He responded by reciting what we know as the Lord's Prayer (Matt. 6:9-13). Jesus began His prayer with a very intimate title for God. In doing so, Jesus reminded us that we, as Christians, have an intimate relationship with God. Yet many believers might have trouble addressing God this way because of past experiences with our earthly fathers.

If our past experiences with our earthly fathers or other authority figures were negative, there's a temptation to associate those characteristics to our relationship with God. Acknowledging God as our Father reminds us that regardless of who our earthly fathers are or were, we have a heavenly Father who loves, provides for, and plans good for us. For us to have

a correct understanding of God the Father, we have to come to know and understand His character by the way He reveals Himself to us in the Scriptures.

God is the perfect Father. He is a God of compassion and mercy. Once we know the Father through His Son, Jesus Christ, we can go to Him anywhere, anytime, and about anything in life. Through grace and faith in Christ, not only does He bring us into His kingdom; He brings us into His family, and we are now His adopted sons and daughters. As you read the assigned Scriptures this week, ask yourself: What does this passage teach me about God? How does it instruct my prayer life? Am I obeying this Scripture? If not, what changes do I need to make? Journal your answers and reflections.

DAY 1
PSALM 103:10-14

_____

_____

_____

_____

_____

_____

_____

_____

_____

DAY 2
ROMANS 2:4

DAY 3
PSALM 86:15

DAY 4
EPHESIANS 2:4-5

_____
_____
_____
_____
_____
_____
_____
_____
_____

DAY 5
2 CORINTHIANS 1:3-4

_____
_____
_____
_____
_____
_____
_____
_____
_____

OUR FATHER IN HEAVEN
THE ADOPTED CHILDREN

The starting point for approaching God as Christ followers is summed up in this single word: Father. Because that word is loaded with preconceived notions for all of us, depending on our relationships with our earthly fathers, praying in this way can be either extraordinarily comforting or extraordinarily problematic. Part of our growth in Christ, as well as our growth in prayer, involves recovering the meaning of this word as it's applied to God.

What does it mean to call God Father? It means, first and foremost, recognizing that addressing God like this in prayer is a unique privilege for Christians. Because all of us have been born in sin, we're separated from our holy God. Far from being our Father, we're His enemies—opposed to Him—for in our sin we would much rather live under our own authority than His.

But when we believe the gospel, He who was once our enemy becomes our Father. We who were once orphans are brought into God's family. Because of the sacrifice of Jesus and our belief in Him, we have a place at God's table. As you read the assigned Scriptures this week, ask yourself: What does this passage teach me about God? How does it instruct my prayer life? Am I obeying this Scripture? If not, what changes do I need to make? Journal your answers and reflections.

DAY 1
1 JOHN 3:1

DAY 2
EPHESIANS 1:3-6

DAY 3
EPHESIANS 1:7-10

DAY 4
EPHESIANS 1:11-14

_____
_____
_____
_____
_____
_____
_____
_____
_____

DAY 5
JOHN 1:12

_____
_____
_____
_____
_____
_____
_____
_____
_____

OUR FATHER IN HEAVEN
THE APPROACHABLE FATHER

When Jesus told His first followers to address God as Father, it must have come as a shock. It wasn't the first shocking thing He had said to them, for the Lord's prayer comes in the context of Jesus' great Sermon on the Mount. Jesus had warmed up the crowd with controversial statements about what it really means to be called blessed and with the assertion that thinking badly of people is the same as killing them. But the introduction of the word Father took the sermon to another level.

Judaism strongly held to the established belief that God was absolutely unapproachable. Was He to be loved? Certainly. Respected? Absolutely. Feared? Without question. This was the culture that wouldn't even speak the revealed name of God, and

when people had to write it in Scripture, they did so with great honor and respect.

Enter Jesus, this strange rabbi who had no fear of or regard for the religious leaders of the time and who spoke with unmatched authority. There He was on a hillside talking about the revered God of Israel with an air of unmistakable familiarity. And that's just what God was going for. God intends for His children to know Him and feel comfortable approaching Him.

As you read the assigned Scriptures this week, ask yourself: What does this passage teach me about God? How does it instruct my prayer life? Am I obeying this Scripture? If not, what changes do I need to make? Journal your answers and reflections.

DAY 1
JAMES 4:8

_____

_____

_____

_____

_____

_____

_____

_____

DAY 4
MATTHEW 7:7–8

_____
_____
_____
_____
_____
_____
_____
_____
_____

DAY 5
ISAIAH 55:6

_____
_____
_____
_____
_____
_____
_____
_____
_____

OUR FATHER IN HEAVEN
THE LOVING FATHER

When Jesus preached the Sermon on the Mount and spoke of the Father with great familiarity, it wasn't that God's purpose was to be disrespected or approached casually—far from it. It was that God wanted to be in a relationship with His people that wasn't marked by fear but by love, not by apprehension but by an appreciation of His great grace and compassion. He wanted to be their dad.

That's where the love of God takes us. John described it like this: "See what great love the Father has given us that we should be called God's children" (1 John 3:1a). God's great love doesn't make us His servants. It doesn't make us the people He puts up with. God's great love makes us His sons and daughters. Father is the Christian name for God.

A real father cares. He protects. He encourages. He advises. But above all, a real father loves. Always and without condition. A real father waits on the porch to welcome home his children, regardless of where they've been or what they've done. A real father is proud of his children and takes no greater pleasure than giving them what they need. Regardless of our relationship with our earthly fathers—as believers in Jesus Christ—we have the opportunity to be fathered by our perfect and loving heavenly Father. As you read the assigned Scriptures this week, ask yourself: What does this passage teach me about God? How does it instruct my prayer life? Am I obeying this Scripture? If not, what changes do I need to make? Journal your answers and reflections.

DAY 1
ROMANS 5:8

_____
_____
_____
_____
_____
_____
_____
_____
_____

DAY 3
PSALM 89:33

_____
_____
_____
_____
_____
_____
_____
_____
_____

DAY 4
JEREMIAH 31:3

_____
_____
_____
_____
_____
_____
_____
_____
_____

DAY 5
PSALM 136:1-5

_____
_____
_____
_____
_____
_____
_____
_____
_____

OUR FATHER IN HEAVEN
THE SPIRIT WHO REMINDS

It's amazing and miraculous to think that we, as sinful humans, can know God as our Father. This reality could be accomplished only by the death and resurrection of Jesus Christ. Because of the gospel, we now know God as Father, and He relates to us as His beloved children.

God is very concerned that we understand and remember the nature of our relationship with Him. For this reason, one of the primary functions of the Holy Spirit is to remind us of the reality of our Father's closeness.

This function of the Holy Spirit is very different from the one many of us tend to think of. Many of us think of the Spirit of God as the voice in our heads that constantly tells us to stop doing what we know is wrong or to start doing more of what

we know is right. We think of Him as the source of the refrain of guilt inside our heads saying either "No! No! No!" or "More! More! More!"

While the Holy Spirit lives inside us to convict us of sin and righteousness, another big role is to remind us of our true identity. He's there to whisper to us over and over, "You're a child of God. He's your Father." This week we'll look at Scriptures that teach us about the role of the Holy Spirit in our lives. As you read the assigned Scriptures this week, ask yourself: What does this passage teach me about God? How does it instruct my prayer life? Am I obeying this Scripture? If not, what changes do I need to make? Journal your answers and reflections.

DAY 1
ROMANS 8:14–16

DAY 2
JOHN 14:26

_____
_____
_____
_____
_____
_____
_____
_____
_____

DAY 3
ROMANS 8:26-27

_____
_____
_____
_____
_____
_____
_____
_____
_____

_____

_____

_____

_____

_____

_____

_____

_____

_____

_____

_____

_____

_____

_____

_____

_____

_____

_____

OUR FATHER IN HEAVEN
THE FATHER WHO'S RIGHT

When we reach out to God as our Father, we recognize that certain realities are baked into that designation. When we call God Father, we're implicitly saying He's loving. We're also saying He's a provider. We're saying He's wise. These are characteristics that all fathers—and certainly our heavenly Father—should embody. But fathers other than God fall short in all of these attributes. They may desire to be perfectly loving, they may strive to be faithful providers, and they may aspire to be perfectly wise, but fathers, like the rest of us, are broken people. Despite their best efforts, they always fall short. But not God. He is the Father who always makes right decisions.

It's important for us to be confident that God will make the right decision on our behalf, because often we don't. For example, we might come to God in prayer asking for something. What we're asking for might be, in our view, the best thing for us. But because God is perfect in His wisdom and fatherhood, He knows there's another side to what we're asking for that will actually harm us.

To approach God as Father is to acknowledge that He knows what's best for us. He's a good Father who is committed to our well-being. As you read the assigned Scriptures this week, ask yourself: What does this passage teach me about God? How does it instruct my prayer life? Am I obeying this Scripture? If not, what changes do I need to make? Journal your answers and reflections.

DAY 1
MATTHEW 7:9-11

_____

_____

_____

_____

_____

_____

_____

_____

_____

DAY 3
PSALM 145:7

_____

_____

_____

_____

_____

_____

_____

_____

_____

DAY 4
DANIEL 2:21-22

_____
_____
_____
_____
_____
_____
_____
_____
_____

DAY 5
ROMANS 11:33-36

_____
_____
_____
_____
_____
_____
_____
_____
_____

OUR FATHER IN HEAVEN
OUR IDENTITY AS CHILDREN OF GOD

If you attend any social gathering where you'll be introduced to new people, you'll undoubtedly be asked what you do for a living, if you're married or single, whether or not you have children, and where you live. Maybe these questions are simply the standard we use to gather background information, or perhaps it's how we size one another up. Either way, these are the questions we tend to ask and answer.

Lofty job titles, advanced degrees, successful spouses, and thriving children all serve as positive social capital. Of course, none of those things tell us much about a person's character or who they really are, but these are the measuring sticks we use.

If we aren't careful, these are the measuring sticks we'll use to define ourselves—and that's a mistake.

As followers of Christ, our worth is found in being children of God. Jesus provides the measure of significance we are looking for. There's nothing wrong with lofty titles, advanced degrees, and flourishing families. If you're blessed with any of these things, you should give thanks to God for them. But none of these things are necessary qualities to be a child of the King. Because of Jesus' work on our behalf, we are free from the pressure to impress or prove anything. As you read the assigned Scriptures this week, ask yourself: What does this passage teach me about God? How does it instruct my prayer life? Am I obeying this Scripture? If not, what changes do I need to make? Journal your answers and reflections.

DAY 1
COLOSSIANS 1:13-14

DAY 2
GALATIANS 3:28

_____

_____

_____

_____

_____

_____

_____

_____

DAY 3
GALATIANS 4:6

_____

_____

_____

_____

_____

_____

_____

_____

_____
_____
_____
_____
_____
_____
_____
_____
_____

DAY 5
EPHESIANS 1:5-8

_____
_____
_____
_____
_____
_____
_____
_____
_____

OUR FATHER IN HEAVEN
THE CELEBRATION OF CHILDREN

If God is our Father, then we're His children. This is a wondrous reality, one the children of God should never get over. It's even more amazing to realize that God doesn't reluctantly hear from His children, but instead, He lovingly and enthusiastically welcomes us into His presence.

This truth highlights another difference between our heavenly Father and our earthly fathers. Though our fathers might be good and faithful men who strive to love, provide for, and protect their children, they're also still men. They grow tired and weary. Surely every father shares the experience of having been so tired after a long day at work that he didn't have the energy to laugh, play with, and spend quality time with his children. But not God.

God isn't ashamed for us to call Him our Father; indeed, He celebrates over His children with gladness.

He exuberantly welcomes us into His presence time and time again, and no matter how much joy we might feel there, it doesn't compare to the amount of joy He feels. For a child of God, coming to the Lord in prayer is an opportunity to join God in a celebration. Though we might come to prayer with a heavy heart, burdened by serious trouble, disease, or discouragement, we find our Father waiting there who's exceedingly glad to welcome us into His presence. As you read the assigned Scriptures this week, ask yourself: What does this passage teach me about God? How does it instruct my prayer life? Am I obeying this Scripture? If not, what changes do I need to make? Journal your answers and reflections.

DAY 1
ZEPHANIAH 3:17

_____
_____
_____
_____
_____
_____
_____
_____
_____
_____

DAY 3
LUKE 15:22-24

_____
_____
_____
_____
_____
_____
_____
_____
_____
_____

DAY 4
PSALM 56:9

_____
_____
_____
_____
_____
_____
_____
_____
_____

DAY 5
LUKE 15:7

_____
_____
_____
_____
_____
_____
_____
_____
_____

Section Three

THE WORTHINESS
OF GOD

YOUR NAME BE HONORED AS HOLY
THE REVEALED NAME

Jesus began the Lord's Prayer by reminding His followers to address God as Father. This is the unique privilege of Christians—those who've been made children of God by His grace through Jesus' death and resurrection. But then Jesus continued with the first request in the Lord's Prayer: "Your name be honored as holy" (Matt. 6:9). We should pray that God's name will be honored as holy.

If this request sounds strange to us, it might be because we tend to place less significance on names than people did in biblical times. For us, the name of a person, place, or thing is simply a designation, an identifying label. But when the Bible speaks of a name, it means something much deeper. A name

is a one-word summation of the essence of the person, place, or thing. A person's name is therefore a summary of his or her character. God is worthy of all worship, glory, praise, and honor. All human beings were created to worship and when we fail to worship God we wind up worshiping something else—and that is idolatry. The Bible mentions several names of God that give us insight into His character. As you learn His names that are revealed in the Scriptures, it's a good idea to incorporate them into your prayer life as a means of worship. As you read the assigned Scriptures this week, ask yourself: What does this passage teach me about God? How does it instruct my prayer life? Am I obeying this Scripture? If not, what changes do I need to make? Journal your answers and reflections.

DAY 1
GENESIS 16:13-14

DAY 2
GENESIS 22:13-14

_____
_____
_____
_____
_____
_____
_____
_____
_____
_____

DAY 3
EXODUS 15:26

_____
_____
_____
_____
_____
_____
_____
_____
_____
_____

_____

_____

_____

_____

_____

_____

_____

_____

_____

_____

_____

_____

_____

_____

_____

_____

YOUR NAME BE HONORED AS HOLY
THE HOLY NAME

Jesus said we should pray that God's name—His identity and character—will be honored as holy. Our desire in prayer, first and foremost, should be for the world to understand and honor who God is and what He has done. When we pray for all people everywhere to honor God's name as holy, we're joining a call to worship God that even now is ringing in the heavens.

To be holy is to be separate. Other. Apart. When we describe God as holy, the word sums up everything that makes Him who He is and sets Him apart from us. But this word is more than a characteristic of God; it summarizes all of His characteristics. Therefore, His holiness filters down into everything else we say about Him.

God's love is a holy love. His justice is a holy justice. His wrath is a holy wrath. God's holiness reminds us that God is completely and perfectly pure, without spot or blemish. God is wholly other—different and set apart from us. Jesus said we're to pray that the entire world comes to this recognition. This overarching desire frames the way we continue our prayer. As you read the assigned Scriptures this week, ask yourself: What does this passage teach me about God? How does it instruct my prayer life? Am I obeying this Scripture? If not, what changes do I need to make? Journal your answers and reflections.

DAY 1
ISAIAH 6:1-3

_____

_____

_____

_____

_____

_____

_____

_____

_____

_____

_____

_____

_____

_____

_____

_____

_____

_____

DAY 3
PSALM 29:2

_____

_____

_____

_____

_____

_____

_____

_____

_____

DAY 5
REVELATION 4:8

YOUR NAME BE HONORED AS HOLY
THE GLORIOUS NAME

Jesus taught that as His followers pray, our priority should be the recognition and reverence of God's name in the whole earth. Although we might grow in our commitment to this aim even as we pray for it, we can also be assured that God Himself is committed to the glory of His own name throughout the world. God always acts for His own glory, and this pursuit is not only good and right but also loving.

While any human being who acts in a self-glorifying way is rightly seen as egotistical, boastful, arrogant, and selfish, it's entirely appropriate for God to seek His own glory. That's because of all the beings in the universe, God is the only One who actually deserves the glory. So whenever we hold something higher than God in our hearts, we call that thing an idol.

If God desired something other than His own glory, He would by definition become an idolater.

God's glorious name should be the driving force behind our prayers, just as it's the driving force behind all His actions. For that reason, when we pray, we must ask God to bend our hearts to His ways, to create in us a greater love for His glory and His name so that we truly desire what He desires. As you read the assigned Scriptures this week, ask yourself: What does this passage teach me about God? How does it instruct my prayer life? Am I obeying this Scripture? If not, what changes do I need to make? Journal your answers and reflections.

DAY 1
HABAKKUK 2:14

_____
_____
_____
_____
_____
_____
_____
_____
_____

_____
_____
_____
_____
_____
_____
_____
_____
_____

DAY 4
ROMANS 8:18

_____

_____

_____

_____

_____

_____

_____

_____

DAY 5
1 CORINTHIANS 10:31

_____

_____

_____

_____

_____

_____

_____

_____

YOUR NAME BE HONORED AS HOLY

THE SAVING NAME

The name of God is holy. When we pray, we aren't praying for His name to be holy but for it to be recognized as what it already is. Part of recognizing God's holiness, however, is recognizing that we aren't holy. If God is holy, meaning He's completely other than we are and perfect in every way, then how can we ever live in a right relationship with Him? How can we expect to come to Him in prayer and expect Him to welcome us?

It's only through the gospel that we become acceptable to the holy God. In Christ we're given the great benefit of His righteousness even as He takes our sin on Himself. This is why the name of God is not just holy; it's also the only name under heaven by which we can be saved.

The name of Jesus is certainly recognizable. Indeed, there's no more recognized name throughout all of human history. Politicians, athletes, rulers, generals—all these have names that are remembered in some corner of the globe, but the name of Jesus stands apart from the rest. This name has stood the test of time, spanning geographical, economic, racial, and national barriers. The name of Jesus has universal appeal because it has the power to save. As you read the assigned Scriptures this week, ask yourself: What does this passage teach me about God? How does it instruct my prayer life? Am I obeying this Scripture? If not, what changes do I need to make? Journal your answers and reflections.

DAY 1
JOHN 3:16

_____

_____

_____

_____

_____

_____

_____

_____

_____

_____
_____
_____
_____
_____
_____
_____
_____
_____

DAY 3
ROMANS 8:34

_____
_____
_____
_____
_____
_____
_____
_____
_____

_____
_____
_____
_____
_____
_____
_____
_____
_____

DAY 5
ISAIAH 43:11

_____
_____
_____
_____
_____
_____
_____
_____
_____

YOUR NAME BE HONORED AS HOLY
THE ONLY NAME

Perhaps you've begun to pray for a person, a circumstance, or an area of the world, asking the Lord for His name to be revered, respected, and trusted in that situation. But then your doubt takes hold. You start to second-guess your prayer, recalling that the person you're praying for has heard the gospel many times before and has rejected it. Or as you think about a region of the world, you consider the cultural or religious challenges to honoring God's name there.

You can feel discouraged and even hopeless when you think about those circumstances and your desire for the name of God to be known and loved among those people and in those situations. In those moments we must remember that the desire to extend and honor God's name isn't merely a wish

that Christians entertain; it's actually a promise. Paul wrote that "every knee will bow and every tongue will confess that Christ is Lord" (Phil.2:9-11).

Indeed, the question isn't whether every person will bow down before the Lord Jesus; the only question is when it will happen for each one of us. The world teaches that there are many paths to God, but that's not true. The Bible teaches Jesus is the only way to God (John 14:6). As you read the assigned Scriptures this week, ask yourself: What does this passage teach me about God? How does it instruct my prayer life? Am I obeying this Scripture? If not, what changes do I need to make? Journal your answers and reflections.

DAY 1
JOHN 14:6

_____

_____

_____

_____

_____

_____

_____

_____

_____

DAY 2
ACTS 4:12

DAY 3
PHILIPPIANS 2:9-12

_____
_____
_____
_____
_____
_____
_____
_____
_____

DAY 5
ACTS 2:36

_____
_____
_____
_____
_____
_____
_____
_____
_____

YOUR NAME BE HONORED AS HOLY
WORTHY OF WORSHIP

Worship is a critical component of prayer that is often overlooked and it's important for more than one reason. First, God is worthy of all praise. As human beings, we were created to worship and when we fail to worship God, we wind up worshiping things other than God and we fall into the trap of idolatry. God takes idolatry so seriously He addressed it in the Ten Commandments: "Do not make an idol for yourself, whether in the shape of anything in the heavens above or on the earth below or in the waters under the earth" (Ex. 20:4).

Second, when you begin prayer in worship, it fuels the rest of your prayer life. Why? Because focusing on the attributes of God emphasizes His power and might. Often times we come to

our prayer time overwhelmed with the problems we are facing. As we worship God, and magnify His attributes, in the shadow of God, our problems begin to look small. One of the reasons God calls us to worship Him is because it reminds us of the magnitude of the God we serve and reorients our thinking. As we worship God, we might call Him by the different names He's called in Scripture that speak to His attributes, or we worship Him for a specific way He's working in our life or because how we've seen Him reveal Himself in Scripture. As you read the assigned Scriptures this week, ask yourself: What does this passage teach me about God? How does it instruct my prayer life? Am I obeying this Scripture? If not, what changes do I need to make? Journal your answers and reflections.

DAY 1
1 CHRONICLES 16:29

_____

_____

_____

_____

_____

_____

_____

_____

_____

_____

_____

_____

_____

_____

_____

_____

_____

_____

DAY 4
2 SAMUEL 22:4

_____
_____
_____
_____
_____
_____
_____
_____
_____

DAY 5
PSALM 34:1

_____
_____
_____
_____
_____
_____
_____
_____
_____

YOUR NAME BE HONORED AS HOLY
WORTHY OF THANKS

God invites us to take our needs to Him in prayer and we are foolish if we don't. But how often do we rush into prayer without giving thanks for the ways God has already blessed us? Gratitude is the only appropriate response to the blessings of God, but it's also good for us. When our eyes are open to the blessings of God our thoughts shift from what we lack to the ways God has already provided. During times of struggle, it's especially important to keep our eyes open to all the ways God is working and to give constant thanks for His grace and goodness.

Being thankful shifts our mental focus to what we have and not what we lack. The truth is, we are far more blessed than we realize. Did you wake up this morning? Not everyone who went to bed last night woke up to live another day. Tired of your work?

Imagine yourself unemployed. Are you complaining because it's time to clean your house? Take a drive down to the homeless shelter. The truth is, we are far more blessed than we realize and there's always a good reason to give thanks to God. As you read the assigned Scriptures this week, ask yourself: What does this passage teach me about God? How does it instruct my prayer life? Am I obeying this Scripture? If not, what changes do I need to make? Journal your answers and reflections.

DAY 1
PSALM 9:1

_____

_____

_____

_____

_____

_____

_____

_____

_____

_____

DAY 3
1 THESSALONIANS 5:16-18

_____

_____

_____

_____

_____

_____

_____

_____

_____

_____

_____

_____

_____

_____

_____

_____

_____

DAY 5
PSALM 95:2

_____

_____

_____

_____

_____

_____

_____

_____

YOUR NAME BE HONORED AS HOLY
GOD IS WORTHY

We've spent the last several weeks studying the second line of the Lord's Prayer: "your name be honored as holy." When Jesus taught on prayer, He wanted to teach His followers how important it is to honor the name of God, and make worship, praise, and thanksgiving a regular part of our daily prayer life. The reality is, God is worthy of all praise, glory, and honor.

The apostle Paul teaches the Father has done this on our behalf: "He has rescued us from the domain of darkness and transferred us into the kingdom of the Son he loves. In him we have redemption, the forgiveness of sins" (Col. 1:13-14). That alone is more than enough reason to praise Him all the days of our life!

Our prayers often reveal where our true priorities lie. If we're praying primarily for our own comfort and needs, we're likely focused on ourselves. But if our prayers reveal a desire for God's name and glory to be lifted up, we're following Jesus down the road of self-denial. Our prayer life will always be a result of what we are thinking and feeling internally. If we believe God is worthy of praise, we will be people who worship Him in prayer.

As you read the assigned Scriptures this week, ask yourself: What does this passage teach me about God? How does it instruct my prayer life? Am I obeying this Scripture? If not, what changes do I need to make? Journal your answers and reflections.

DAY 1
1 CHRONICLES 16:23-24

DAY 2
EXODUS 15:2

_____

_____

_____

_____

_____

_____

_____

_____

_____

DAY 3
HEBREWS 13:15

_____

_____

_____

_____

_____

_____

_____

_____

DAY 4
PSALM 150:6

_____
_____
_____
_____
_____
_____
_____
_____

DAY 5
REVELATION 19:1

_____
_____
_____
_____
_____
_____
_____
_____

Section Four

THE KINGDOM AND WILL OF GOD

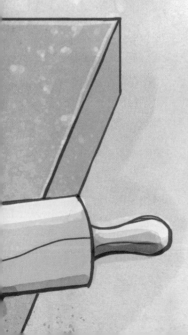

YOUR KINGDOM COME
A GOD-CENTERED PERSPECTIVE

As we continue through our study of the Lord's Prayer, we arrive at the next line of Jesus' prayer: "Your kingdom come. Your will be done on earth as it is in heaven" (Matt. 6:10-11). Just as Jesus pointed to the glory of God in the previous portion of His prayer, He continued with a God-centered perspective. Jesus instructed us to pray that God's kingdom would come and that His will would be done on earth as it is in heaven.

God's kingdom is His rule and reign both in our lives and on the earth, and one day on the new earth. The kingdom comes in our lives when we are surrendered to the will of God, when we're dying each day to our own desires. We pray for the kingdom of God to come and for the will of God to be done,

and then we act in faith by doing the things that are tangible examples of the rule and the reign of God.

When we are asking for the kingdom of God to come in situations of life, then we're asking that the ruling presence of Jesus that already exists would exist in this very moment, for this very season, for this specific time in our life. As you read the assigned Scriptures this week, ask yourself: What does this passage teach me about God? How does it instruct my prayer life? Am I obeying this Scripture? If not, what changes do I need to make? Journal your answers and reflections.

DAY 1
MATTHEW 3:2

_____

_____

_____

_____

_____

_____

_____

_____

_____

DAY 4
MATTHEW 16:19

_____

_____

_____

_____

_____

_____

_____

_____

DAY 5
HEBREWS 1:8

_____

_____

_____

_____

_____

_____

_____

_____

YOUR KINGDOM COME
EMBRACING THE KINGDOM

Having helped us, as His disciples, see the unique privilege of coming to God as our Father, Jesus then taught that our prayers should be dominated by a vision for the name and the glory of God. When Jesus prayed the phrase "Your kingdom come" in the Lord's Prayer, this instruction was directly in line with the entire ministry of Jesus, for He frequently taught on the kingdom of God.

But the very fact that we're to pray for God's kingdom to come and for His will to be done forces us to recognize that although Jesus brought the kingdom to the earth in Himself, the kingdom isn't yet fully realized. The kingdom of God burst into the world in the person of Jesus Christ. He came in power, and His death on the cross conquered death. The end is no longer

in doubt, yet there are still battles to be fought. There's still a kingdom to be advanced. That means we pray for the lost to be saved, for the hungry to be fed, and for the helpless to be protected. In all these ways and more, God will continue to bring His kingdom and will on earth, even as it is in heaven. As you read the assigned Scriptures this week, ask yourself: What does this passage teach me about God? How does it instruct my prayer life? Am I obeying this Scripture? If not, what changes do I need to make? Journal your answers and reflections.

DAY 1
MATTHEW 6:33

_____
_____
_____
_____
_____
_____
_____
_____
_____

_____
_____
_____
_____
_____
_____
_____
_____
_____

DAY 4
JOHN 3:3

_____
_____
_____
_____
_____
_____
_____
_____
_____
_____

DAY 5
I CORINTHIANS 4:20

_____
_____
_____
_____
_____
_____
_____
_____
_____
_____

YOUR KINGDOM COME

UNDERSTANDING GOD'S WILL

"What is God's will for my life?" Most of the time when we ask that question, we want an answer to a specific issue in our lives. We want to know God's will about what job we should pursue, what city we should live in, or whom we should marry.

Jesus told us to pray that as God's kingdom comes on earth, His will would also be done. The accomplishment of God's will fits hand in glove with the coming of His kingdom, for it's in God's kingdom where His will is lovingly and joyfully obeyed. Though it's good and right for us to seek the answers to specific questions, the plain truth is that the vast majority of God's will has already been revealed to us. His Word is full of commands that reveal the way we should live and how we should pray.

The vast majority of us don't need further education on God's will; instead, we need to begin living more fully in what we already know God's will to be. This fact changes the shape of our prayers, both for ourselves and for others. As you read the assigned Scriptures this week, ask yourself: What does this passage teach me about God? How does it instruct my prayer life? Am I obeying this Scripture? If not, what changes do I need to make? Journal your answers and reflections.

DAY 1
PSALM 40:8

DAY 2
MATTHEW 7:21

_____
_____
_____
_____
_____
_____
_____
_____
_____

DAY 3
PSALM 25:4

_____
_____
_____
_____
_____
_____
_____
_____

DAY 4
JOHN 4:34

_____
_____
_____
_____
_____
_____
_____
_____
_____

DAY 5
ROMANS 12:2

_____
_____
_____
_____
_____
_____
_____
_____
_____

YOUR KINGDOM COME
UNDERSTANDING GOD'S WILL FOR MY LIFE

We can apply this line of Jesus' Model Prayer—for God's will to be done—on an individual level. Instead of spending most of our time praying to find out what God's will is, we might pray instead for courage and perseverance to live inside His revealed will. We might pray that we'll be pure. That we'll be faithful husbands and wives. That we'll lovingly and generously serve the church.

In the same way, we can confidently pray for others to be inside God's will. We can ask the Lord for our lost friends and family members to come to know Christ, for we know this is His will. We can pray against systemic injustice that we see around

the world, for we also know that God's will is for justice to reign. We can pray for people in positions of power and authority, knowing that this is God's will too. In short, when we read God's Word, we're reading His will, and that Word can inform us accordingly. As you read the assigned Scriptures this week, ask yourself: What does this passage teach me about God? How does it instruct my prayer life? Am I obeying this Scripture? If not, what changes do I need to make? Journal your answers and reflections.

DAY 1
1 THESSALONIANS 4:3-5

_____

_____

_____

_____

_____

_____

_____

_____

DAY 3
COLOSSIANS 1:9-11

_____

_____

_____

_____

_____

_____

_____

_____

_____
_____
_____
_____
_____
_____
_____
_____
_____

DAY 5
PHILIPPIANS 1:9-11

_____
_____
_____
_____
_____
_____
_____
_____
_____

YOUR KINGDOM COME

JESUS' OBEDIENCE TO GOD'S WILL

Jesus gave us the words of the Lord's Prayer in response to a request from His disciples. They asked Him to teach them how to pray (see Luke 11:1), and that's exactly what the Lord's Prayer does. It's a lesson in prayer. But the Bible shows us more than this lesson; it shows us that Jesus practiced what He preached.

Although the Bible tells us of many occasions when Jesus went off by Himself to pray, perhaps our most vivid picture comes from the night before His crucifixion. Knowing His death was imminent and knowing the suffering He would endure, Jesus approached His Father. The substance of that prayer involved the will of God.

The Bible tells us that during the night, Jesus was in spiritual anguish because of what was coming. He prayed to His Father, asking if there might be another way for His plan of redemption to come to pass. But ultimately, Jesus yielded to the wisdom and authority of His Father (Matt. 26:39).

Submission to the will of God would cost Jesus His life, and it's the same with us. We're giving over our plans, our dreams, and our aspirations to the will of God. As you read the assigned Scriptures this week, ask yourself: What does this passage teach me about God? How does it instruct my prayer life? Am I obeying this Scripture? If not, what changes do I need to make? Journal your answers and reflections.

DAY 1
MATTHEW 26:39

_____

_____

_____

_____

_____

_____

_____

_____

_____

_____

_____

_____

_____

_____

_____

_____

_____

_____

_____

_____

_____

_____

_____

_____

_____

DAY 5
ROMANS 6:16

YOUR KINGDOM COME
SUBMITTING
TO GOD'S WILL

Jesus submitted to the will of God even though He knew the pain, hardship, and suffering it would cause. The same will be true for us. If we want to follow Jesus, it will cost us everything. Just as the cross meant certain death for people who carried it during that time, taking up our cross today means we're giving ourselves over to death. It means every day we're willing to die to ourselves in order to live according to the will of God. This reality should make a forceful impact on us as we pray for the will of God to come to pass.

When we pray for God's will, we're committing ourselves to God's plans rather than our own. We're expressing trust in Him, believing we're dying to the path that might be most comfortable,

profitable, or easy for us because it falls short of God's will for our lives. So we pray for God's will to be done, recognizing that in doing so, we're giving ourselves over to Him. But we do so in faith, believing that those who lose their lives will once again find them in Christ. As you read the assigned Scriptures this week, ask yourself: What does this passage teach me about God? How does it instruct my prayer life? Am I obeying this Scripture? If not, what changes do I need to make? Journal your answers and reflections.

DAY 1
LUKE 9:23-24

DAY 5
ROMANS 6:11

YOUR KINGDOM COME
TRUSTING GOD'S WILL

We all experience times in life when we think God should answer our prayers with a specific outcome and we're disillusioned when He doesn't. It's during times when we don't understand what God is up to that we must rely on what we know to be true about His character. Fortunately for us, God's will is a function of His character. If we believe that God is good, loving, generous, and wise and that He's a Father who always acts in the best interests of His children, we should long for His will to be done. It's because we trust in the character of God, who has shown Himself to be faithful time and time again, that we can trust the will of God.

So even though we might not know what tomorrow holds we can be confident about the future, and we can pray for God's will to come to pass. For Christians, then, praying for God's will to be done is both a matter of great humility and of great boldness at the same time. As you read the assigned Scriptures this week, ask yourself: What does this passage teach me about God? How does it instruct my prayer life? Am I obeying this Scripture? If not, what changes do I need to make? Journal your answers and reflections.

DAY 1
PROVERBS 3:5–6

_____

_____

_____

_____

_____

_____

_____

_____

_____

_____

DAY 3
ISAIAH 40:31

_____

_____

_____

_____

_____

_____

_____

_____

_____

DAY 4
PSALM 19:7

_____
_____
_____
_____
_____
_____
_____
_____
_____

DAY 5
HEBREWS 2:13

_____
_____
_____
_____
_____
_____
_____
_____
_____

YOUR KINGDOM COME
ALREADY, BUT NOT YET

The kingdom of God is an already-but-not-yet reality. Christians are living in that meantime in a spiritual sense. Jesus brought the kingdom with Him, and He secured the ultimate victory for God's kingdom through His death and resurrection. But that victory won't be fully realized until Jesus returns. In the meantime, Christians are the representatives of the kingdom of God on earth. That means the values, priorities, and goals of the kingdom should be fully represented in the church. When people look at the church, they should see a visual representation of what the kingdom of God will be like when Jesus comes back.

When will that happen? We don't know, and Jesus isn't concerned that we know. Instead, He's concerned that we're busy with the work of God's kingdom, praying and working for

it to come in power, right now in the meantime. Jesus' followers today might easily be consumed with the timing of God's kingdom. We know someday Jesus is going to return, and His victory will be consummated here on earth. Yet He left work for us to do in the here and now. Rather than concerning ourselves with when, we should be concerned with what. Therefore, our prayers should focus on sharing the gospel in all corners of the globe and completing the mission Jesus gave to His followers. As you read the assigned Scriptures this week, ask yourself: What does this passage teach me about God? How does it instruct my prayer life? Am I obeying this Scripture? If not, what changes do I need to make? Journal your answers and reflections.

DAY 1
ACTS 1:7-8

_____

_____

_____

_____

_____

_____

_____

_____

_____

DAY 3
COLOSSIANS 4:3

_____

_____

_____

_____

_____

_____

_____

_____

_____

_____

_____

_____

_____

_____

_____

_____

_____

_____

_____

_____

_____

_____

_____

_____

_____

_____

_____

_____

_____

Section Five

THE PROVISION OF GOD

GIVE US TODAY OUR DAILY BREAD
OUR PROVIDER

Up until this point in the Lord's Prayer, Jesus focused on the name and glory of God and His kingdom. This is instructive for us, because it teaches us that prayer isn't only about getting our needs met but is primarily about the glory of God. Even as Jesus shifts the subject to focus on our specific needs, He does so by acknowledging our weakness and need to trust God. In light of that, Jesus told God we should ask, "Give us today our daily bread" (Matt. 6:11). When we ask for daily bread, what we're saying is, "God, You're the source of everything good in my life, and You've created my body with needs."

God is our provider. Whether or not we recognize it, we're dependent on Him each day to give us everything we need.

When we pray like this daily, we acknowledge that God alone can fulfill all of our needs and satisfy us. We also humbly accept we can't provide for ourselves. We should pray as if everything depends on God—because it does. As you read the assigned Scriptures this week, ask yourself: What does this passage teach me about God? How does it instruct my prayer life? Am I obeying this Scripture? If not, what changes do I need to make? Journal your answers and reflections.

DAY 1
PSALM 34:10

_____

_____

_____

_____

_____

_____

_____

_____

_____
_____
_____
_____
_____
_____
_____
_____

_____
_____
_____
_____
_____
_____
_____
_____
_____

_____
_____
_____
_____
_____
_____
_____
_____
_____

DAY 5
1 CORINTHIANS 4:7

_____
_____
_____
_____
_____
_____
_____
_____
_____

GIVE US TODAY OUR DAILY BREAD
BREAD FROM HEAVEN

Jesus told us we should pray like this: "Give us today our daily bread" (Matt. 6:11). Jesus used the metaphor of bread, the most basic provision for His audience, to say we should ask God to give us what we need to live and thrive in daily life. This request recalls the time during the exodus when God provided for His people in the wilderness. Having been miraculously delivered from slavery in Egypt, the Israelites crossed the Red Sea under Moses' leadership. But despite witnessing the wonders of God, they soon drifted into fear and complaining (Ex.16:3). In response, God provided what the people needed, giving them bread from heaven, but He instructed them to only gather what they needed for that day.

The people soon found that God was very serious about the specific nature of His command, for when they gathered more than they needed, the bread from heaven bred worms and stank. This is a powerful lesson for both the children of Israel and the children of God today. When Jesus told us to ask for our bread and to do it daily, He was reminding us that only God can provide what we need. So when we pray this portion of the Lord's Prayer, we're not only expressing our trust in God to give us what we need to survive; we're also acknowledging our own weakness and our dependence on God's gracious provision to give us life. As you read the assigned Scriptures this week, ask yourself: What does this passage teach me about God? How does it instruct my prayer life? Am I obeying this Scripture? If not, what changes do I need to make? Journal your answers and reflections.

DAY 1
PSALM 16:2

_____

_____

_____

_____

_____

_____

_____

_____

_____

_____

_____

_____

_____

_____

_____

_____

_____

_____

_____
_____
_____
_____
_____
_____
_____
_____
_____

_____
_____
_____
_____
_____
_____
_____
_____
_____

GIVE US TODAY OUR DAILY BREAD
THE WORD OF THE LORD

When we ask the Lord each day to give us the bread we need, we're expressing confidence in His willingness and ability to provide what we need. We're simultaneously acknowledging our abject dependence on Him for the very fabric of our lives. God, as the great and generous giver, receives glory when He provides what we need. But what do we really need? What's this bread we're praying for? Certainly it means the basic necessities of life like food, water, shelter, and even the breath in our lungs. And yet there's more, because as Jesus would teach us, we don't live on bread alone (Matt. 4:3-4).

When we come to God asking for our daily bread, we should be aware that our true need is in our souls. We need God and

His Word to tell us who He is, who we are, the nature of life and the universe, and how we're supposed to live. As we pray for our daily bread, we can and should trust God to provide for us physically. At the same time, we should pray for and give thanks for His willingness to meet our greatest needs—the needs that go beyond physical hunger to the spiritual hunger for Him that all of us have. As you read the assigned Scriptures this week, ask yourself: What does this passage teach me about God? How does it instruct my prayer life? Am I obeying this Scripture? If not, what changes do I need to make? Journal your answers and reflections.

DAY 1
PSALM 23:1

_____

_____

_____

_____

_____

_____

_____

_____

_____

_____

_____

_____

_____

_____

_____

_____

_____

_____

DAY 3
PSALM 119:92

_____

_____

_____

_____

_____

_____

_____

_____

_____

_____
_____
_____
_____
_____
_____
_____
_____
_____

_____
_____
_____
_____
_____
_____
_____
_____
_____

GIVE US TODAY OUR DAILY BREAD
THE DAY GOD HAS MADE

No one knows for certain what today holds. This might be a day of great joy or immense sadness; it might be a day of opportunity or a day of rejection; it might be a day of laughter or a day of tears. We simply don't know for sure. How wonderful, then, to know that even though we suffer from an almost paralyzing lack of knowledge, the Lord knows our end before our beginning (Isa. 46:10). Though we don't know what today holds, God certainly does.

How should we respond to that knowledge? In prayer we respond by confidently asking the Lord to give us what we need even though we don't know exactly what we need. But because we trust in His good character and correspondingly

good provision, we can rejoice, for we're confident that this day, no matter what it holds, is the day God has made for us.

Rejoicing in the day God has made means embracing the sovereign work of a loving God instead of wishing for another one. It means when we pray for our daily bread, we can do so with both joy and confidence. As you read the assigned Scriptures this week, ask yourself: What does this passage teach me about God? How does it instruct my prayer life? Am I obeying this Scripture? If not, what changes do I need to make? Journal your answers and reflections.

DAY 1
PSALM 118:24

DAY 3
PSALM 16:9

_____

_____

_____

_____

_____

_____

_____

_____

_____

_____

_____

_____

_____

_____

_____

_____

_____

_____

GIVE US TODAY OUR DAILY BREAD
THE NEED FOR CONTENTMENT

It's notable that Jesus taught us to pray, "Give us today our daily bread" because bread is very basic in nature (Matt. 6:11). For thousands of years, it has been one of the basic staples of life. But although bread provides what we might need for a given meal, it doesn't necessarily provide exactly what we want.

Consider the Israelites during the exodus. When the bread fell down from heaven, at first they were satisfied. But eventually, the bread grew boring to their taste buds, so they once again complained against Moses and the Lord (Num. 21:5). There's a considerable difference between what we need and what we want. When we pray, then, we should be careful not to assume that praying for God to give us our daily bread means trusting that He will fulfill every one of our wants in exactly the way we

think He should. If that were the case, God would function more like a cosmic butler than a heavenly Father. Receiving our daily bread from God requires us to understand contentment. We must actively choose contentment when we consider God's provision, believing He has given us the right thing at the right time. As you read the assigned Scriptures this week, ask yourself: What does this passage teach me about God? How does it instruct my prayer life? Am I obeying this Scripture? If not, what changes do I need to make? Journal your answers and reflections.

DAY 1
EXODUS 16:8

_____
_____
_____
_____
_____
_____
_____
_____
_____

_____
_____
_____
_____
_____
_____
_____
_____
_____

DAY 4
PSALM 63:5

_____
_____
_____
_____
_____
_____
_____
_____
_____

DAY 5
PSALM 81:10

_____
_____
_____
_____
_____
_____
_____
_____
_____

GIVE US TODAY OUR DAILY BREAD
THE SECRET TO CONTENTMENT

The apostle Paul understood the secret to contentment. He wrote: "I don't say this out of need, for I have learned to be content in whatever circumstance I find myself. I know both how to make do with little, and I know how to make do with a lot. In any and all circumstances I have learned the secret of being content—whether well fed or hungry, whether in abundance or need. I am able to do all things through him who strengthens me" (Phil. 4:11-13).

Verse 13 is often quoted. We misunderstand its meaning, though, when we use this verse in a triumphant sense to claim that Jesus will help us conquer any foe or meet any challenge. The context indicates that Paul was specifically addressing the

issue of contentment. Here was a man, as he himself said, who knew what it meant to have little and to have plenty, to be well fed and to be hungry. And through Christ he could be content with whatever the Lord saw fit to give him on a given day. But we can't muster this kind of contentment on our own. Our faith must be not only in God, who gives us our daily bread, but also in Jesus, who gives us strength to be content with God's provision. As you read the assigned Scriptures this week, ask yourself: What does this passage teach me about God? How does it instruct my prayer life? Am I obeying this Scripture? If not, what changes do I need to make? Journal your answers and reflections.

DAY 1
PHILIPPIANS 4:11-13

_____

_____

_____

_____

_____

_____

_____

_____

_____

_____

_____

_____

_____

_____

_____

_____

_____

_____

DAY 4
ISAIAH 55:2

DAY 5
ISAIAH 58:11

GIVE US TODAY OUR DAILY BREAD

HOW MUCH IS TOO MUCH?

As citizens living in the most prosperous nation in the world, we are routinely bombarded with advertisements intended to send messages about what we "need" and what will make us happy. While there's nothing wrong with owning things—a mindful Christian must ask, "How much is too much?"

The Bible has a lot to say about managing money and possessions. The Bible teaches that money is neutral—it's neither good nor evil. But the Scriptures do teach that the love of money is evil (1 Tim. 6:10). The way we manage our possessions reveals a lot about the state of our heart. Do we look to our possessions, bank accounts, and 401K rather than God as our source of security? Do we work ourselves to death to make more money and ignore our physical and spiritual health?

Do we spend money on things we don't need and ignore God's command to tithe?

The Bible doesn't explicitly answer the question, "How much is too much?" But it has plenty to say about how to manage our resources in a way that honors God and keeps us free from the trap of materialism. As you read the assigned Scriptures this week, ask yourself: What does this passage teach me about God? How does it instruct my prayer life? Am I obeying this Scripture? If not, what changes do I need to make? Journal your answers and reflections.

DAY 1
MATTHEW 6:19-20

_____

_____

_____

_____

_____

_____

_____

_____

_____

_____

_____

_____

_____

_____

_____

_____

_____

DAY 3
MALACHI 3:8-11

_____

_____

_____

_____

_____

_____

_____

_____

_____

_____

_____

_____

_____

_____

_____

_____

DAY 5
2 CORINTHIANS 9:6-7

_____

_____

_____

_____

_____

_____

_____

_____

_____

GIVE US TODAY OUR DAILY BREAD
THE GOD WHO PROVIDES

Our God provides. That statement is straightforward enough, yet we still feel a measure of anxiety and worry when we think about the future. Will we have enough money? Will we get sick? Will we have a place to live? These are legitimate questions, yet we can take each one of them again and again to the Lord in prayer. And again and again we can ask the Lord to "give us today our daily bread" (Matt. 6:11).

How then do we fight anxiety when we're worried about provision for the future? In prayer we can remember the storehouses of God, acknowledging that He doesn't lack anything and therefore has infinite resources at His disposal. At the same time, we can call to mind specific instances from our past when God provided in big and small ways. When we recall

ways God has provided for us in the past, it builds our faith that He will continue to provide for our future needs. We all have a history with God and it's wise for us to rehearse God's past faithfulness. Having done these things, not only can we pray for what we need on a given day, but we can also do so with confidence in the God who gives the daily bread we need. As you read the assigned Scriptures this week, ask yourself: What does this passage teach me about God? How does it instruct my prayer life? Am I obeying this Scripture? If not, what changes do I need to make? Journal your answers and reflections.

DAY 1
PHILIPPIANS 4:19-20

_____

_____

_____

_____

_____

_____

_____

_____

_____

DAY 5
PSALM 77:11

_____

_____

_____

_____

_____

_____

_____

_____

_____

Section Six

THE FORGIVENESS
OF GOD

FORGIVE US OUR DEBTS

A PETITION FOR FORGIVENESS

The next lines of the Lord's Prayer deal with forgiveness:

Forgive us our debts,

as we also have forgiven our debtors.

Matthew 6:12

Jesus said we should ask God to forgive us as we have forgiven our debtors. Clearly, there's a link between our forgiveness of others and God's forgiveness of us. What's that link? And why should we pray for forgiveness if Christ has already forgiven us?

For us to ever come into the presence of a perfectly holy God and feel like we don't need forgiveness would be the greatest sense of arrogance. When we ask for forgiveness of our sins, we're expressing faith in God's mercy. Our ongoing petition

for forgiveness is an opportunity for God, again and again, to remind us of the good news of the gospel. It's also a chance for us, again and again, to humble ourselves before Him and declare that we need His mercy.

When I think about all that Christ did for me on the cross by taking my sins, bearing my shame, my guilt, in His body on that tree, how can I not forgive someone who's done something against me? No matter what somebody may have done to you, they have not done to you what your sin did to Jesus. As you read the assigned Scriptures this week, ask yourself: What does this passage teach me about God? How does it instruct my prayer life? Am I obeying this Scripture? If not, what changes do I need to make? Journal your answers and reflections.

DAY 1
PSALM 130:4

_____

_____

_____

_____

_____

_____

_____

_____

_____

DAY 4
LUKE 23:34

_____
_____
_____
_____
_____
_____
_____
_____
_____

DAY 5
COLOSSIANS 2:13

_____
_____
_____
_____
_____
_____
_____
_____
_____

FORGIVE US OUR DEBTS
THE CONDEMNED SINNER

When we pray, we come into the presence of a holy God. This is a fearful prospect, for when we come into His presence, our sin is starkly exposed. Time and time again in the Old Testament when people met with God, they assumed a humble and even terrified posture, not only because of God's power but also because in His presence they realized with vivid, startling clarity the depth of their sin. The holiness of God brings to light the sin of human beings. This is true without exception, for we are sinners without exception.

No one can stand in the presence of a holy God. No one can claim righteousness when they see what righteousness truly is. Any excuses crumble in God's presence. There's no bartering or trading, for the only thing we bring into the presence of God is

our own need—for provision, for care, but most profoundly for forgiveness.

Asking God for forgiveness of our debts, or sins, isn't a one-time plea but a petition we make over and over again, for although we've been made righteous in Christ, we nonetheless commit acts of rebellion daily. We fail to live as the righteous sons and daughters God has declared us to be in Christ. As you read the assigned Scriptures this week, ask yourself: What does this passage teach me about God? How does it instruct my prayer life? Am I obeying this Scripture? If not, what changes do I need to make? Journal your answers and reflections.

DAY 1
ROMANS 3:23

DAY 2
1 TIMOTHY 1:15

_____

_____

_____

_____

_____

_____

_____

_____

_____

_____

DAY 3
MATTHEW 9:13

_____

_____

_____

_____

_____

_____

_____

_____

_____

_____

_____
_____
_____
_____
_____
_____
_____
_____
_____

DAY 5
PSALM 1:1–2

_____
_____
_____
_____
_____
_____
_____
_____
_____

FORGIVE US OUR DEBTS
A CONTINUAL PLEA

When we pray, then, we should make it our practice to ask for forgiveness. We should do so not only in a general sense but also specifically. We should confess specific instances of jealousy, anger, lust, lying, cheating, and every other way we've fallen short of God's holy standard.

We don't confess our sins to give God information. He knows better than we do the full extent of our sin. Nor do we confess our sins because God withholds His forgiveness until we ask for it. Once we've come into right-standing with God through Christ and His sacrifice, God has forgiven our sins— past, present, and future.

We confess our sins to the Lord for the sake of our relationship with Him. God desires that we live in a love relationship with Him. He wants us to obey Him but to do so out of love for Him. Because we love God and because we know He loves us, we confess sin. We don't want anything, known but unspoken, to come between us and our heavenly Father. We confess our sins so that our hearts can be unburdened and we can be reminded again of God's limitless, gracious love for us. As you read the assigned Scriptures this week, ask yourself: What does this passage teach me about God? How does it instruct my prayer life? Am I obeying this Scripture? If not, what changes do I need to make? Journal your answers and reflections.

DAY 1
1 JOHN 1:9

_____

_____

_____

_____

_____

_____

_____

_____

_____

_____

_____

_____

_____

_____

_____

_____

_____

_____

DAY 4
PSALM 51:1-3

_____
_____
_____
_____
_____
_____
_____
_____
_____

DAY 5
PSALM 51:4-10

_____
_____
_____
_____
_____
_____
_____
_____
_____

FORGIVE US OUR DEBTS
THE FORGIVING GOD

It's difficult to ask for forgiveness. When we know we've wronged someone, we're much more likely to remain silent and ignore the issue, hoping it will go away. Why do we do this?

Part of the reason is that it's inherently humbling to ask for forgiveness. When you truly ask for forgiveness, you're throwing yourself on the mercy of another person. You're confessing that you need something only they can grant, and it's entirely up to them whether to forgive you. In short, asking forgiveness removes the power of relationship from us and gives it to someone else.

This situation can be disconcerting because you don't know how the other person will respond. You don't know whether they'll be favorable and gracious or bitter and angry. They might

assure you of their ongoing love, or they might tell you to keep your apology. Yet this ambiguity is one reason God's forgiveness is a powerful reminder of the gospel.

When we come to God, asking Him to forgive us when we've wronged Him, we can be assured of His response. We don't have to wonder whether we've outsinned His grace or overstayed our welcome in His family. We're secure in Christ, and based on the foundation of that security, we can know with glorious confidence how the Lord will respond when we humbly approach Him and ask for forgiveness. As you read the assigned Scriptures this week, ask yourself: What does this passage teach me about God? How does it instruct my prayer life? Am I obeying this Scripture? If not, what changes do I need to make? Journal your answers and reflections.

DAY 1
PSALM 103:1-5

DAY 2
PSALM 103:6-10

DAY 3
PSALM 103:11-16

_____

_____

_____

_____

_____

_____

_____

_____

_____

_____

_____

_____

_____

_____

_____

_____

FORGIVE US OUR DEBTS
THE HONEST CONFESSION

Jesus' instruction in the Lord's Prayer to confess our sins reminds us that we always have sins to confess. The apostle John expressed it this way:

If we say, "We have no sin," we are deceiving ourselves, and the truth is not in us. If we confess our sins, he is faithful and righteous to forgive us our sins and to cleanse us from all unrighteousness (1 John 1:8-9).

These verses contain both a universal truth and a powerful promise. The truth is that all of us have not only sinned but we have also sinned recently. Even today. Perhaps in the last few minutes. This is because although we've been made new in Christ, the remnants of our old self remain. The pull of sin is strong and appealing, and far too often we choose to walk

according to those sinful desires instead of walking according to the Holy Spirit who lives in us (see Rom. 8:5).

This is a universal truth. If we deny that we've sinned, John tells us we're delusional. But these verses also contain a wonderful promise. As sure as the fact that we all sin is the fact that God is "faithful and righteous" (v. 9) to forgive us of that sin. When we humbly come to the Lord who loves us, having given His one and only Son as the substitute for our sin, we can know with certainty that He has forgiven us and will forgive us. As you read the assigned Scriptures this week, ask yourself: What does this passage teach me about God? How does it instruct my prayer life? Am I obeying this Scripture? If not, what changes do I need to make? Journal your answers and reflections.

DAY 1
PSALM 32:5

DAY 4
NEHEMIAH 1:6

_____
_____
_____
_____
_____
_____
_____
_____
_____

DAY 5
PROVERBS 28:13

_____
_____
_____
_____
_____
_____
_____
_____
_____

FORGIVE US OUR DEBTS

A WILLINGNESS TO FORGIVE

God's overwhelming willingness to forgive has great implications for believers. Because God forgives us without limit, we can live in freedom. We should want to please Him. Our lives should be filled with an ongoing sense of gratitude when we live in this forgiveness. But one of the strongest implications of God's forgiveness is our willingness to forgive other people. Jesus knew this necessity well. That's why in the Lord's Prayer He linked God's forgiveness with our willingness to forgive others.

Forgive us our debts,
as we also have forgiven our debtors.
Matthew 6:12

At first reading, we might think Jesus was stating that God's forgiveness is proportionate to our forgiveness of others. But this prayer doesn't mean God will forgive us only when we forgive other people. It's saying that our willingness to forgive other people reflects what we perceive God's forgiveness of us to be like. This is a difficult truth to grasp because we all love to be forgiven, yet we find it difficult to do the same when others have wronged us. For us to forgive others as God commands, we need to ask for His grace to do so. As you read the assigned Scriptures this week, ask yourself: What does this passage teach me about God? How does it instruct my prayer life? Am I obeying this Scripture? If not, what changes do I need to make? Journal your answers and reflections.

DAY 1
GENESIS 32:20

_____

_____

_____

_____

_____

_____

_____

_____

_____

DAY 3
EXODUS 34:9

_____

_____

_____

_____

_____

_____

_____

_____

_____

DAY 4
1 SAMUEL 25:28

_____

_____

_____

_____

_____

_____

_____

_____

_____

DAY 5
ACTS 26:18

_____

_____

_____

_____

_____

_____

_____

_____

_____

FORGIVE US OUR DEBTS
HOW MANY TIMES MUST I FORGIVE?

Forgiving others is difficult. It was certainly difficult for Peter, who pressed Jesus in Matthew 18 to learn the extent to which he had to forgive those who wronged him. Jesus had just finished teaching on the process of confrontation when a fellow Christian sins against us. Peter, hearing Jesus' emphasis on honest, direct communication with the aim of restoration, came back with what he considered a very generous offer: "Lord, how many times shall I forgive my brother or sister who sins against me? As many as seven times?" (Matt. 18:21)

The rabbis of the day taught that three instances of forgiveness were sufficient. Peter went beyond that. He volunteered to forgive someone up to seven times, going well beyond what was

culturally expected. But Jesus wiped the smugness off Peter's face with His next statement: "I tell you, not as many as seven, … but seventy times seven" (Matt. 18:22).

Jesus' point was clear: there's no specific limit to the number of times you should forgive another person; instead, you should generously forgive as God has forgiven you. But we'll need to rely on God's grace to forgive others repeatedly. The good news is His grace abounds. As you read the assigned Scriptures this week, ask yourself: What does this passage teach me about God? How does it instruct my prayer life? Am I obeying this Scripture? If not, what changes do I need to make? Journal your answers and reflections.

DAY 1
MATTHEW 18:21-22

_____
_____
_____
_____
_____
_____
_____
_____
_____

_____
_____
_____
_____
_____
_____
_____
_____
_____

DAY 4
2 CORINTHIANS 1:12

DAY 5
2 CORINTHIANS 6:1

FORGIVE US OUR DEBTS
FORGIVEN PEOPLE FORGIVE

As we've studied the nature of forgiveness through the lens of the Lord's Prayer, it's clear that forgiven people forgive people. It's that simple. But the reverse is also true. When we find ourselves absolutely unwilling to forgive, it reveals that we don't comprehend the great debt of which God has forgiven us. Our lack of forgiveness shows that in our pride we don't consider ourselves to be truly in debt to God because our sin was either not that grievous or not that extensive. Nothing could be further from the truth.

Our sin cost Jesus His life. Our sin was so great that the required payment was the sacrifice of God's own Son. Knowing the devastating nature of our offenses, how could we withhold forgiveness from another person? As we pray, we must pray

with one eye on our own sin and one eye on our brother's. We must make sure we aren't so arrogant as to ask God for His forgiveness while we're withholding forgiveness from someone else. The parable of the unforgiving servant in Matthew 18:23-35 illustrates this point and it would be beneficial to include in your reading. As you read the assigned Scriptures this week, ask yourself: What does this passage teach me about God? How does it instruct my prayer life? Am I obeying this Scripture? If not, what changes do I need to make? Journal your answers and reflections.

DAY 1
MATTHEW 18:32-33

DAY 3
LUKE 7:47

DAY 4
MATTHEW 5:7

_____

_____

_____

_____

_____

_____

_____

_____

_____

DAY 5
JAMES 2:13

_____

_____

_____

_____

_____

_____

_____

_____

_____

Section Seven

THE PROTECTION OF GOD

DO NOT BRING US INTO TEMPTATION
YOU HAVE AN ENEMY

In Jesus' concluding statement in the Lord's Prayer, He instructed us to pray:

> Do not bring us into temptation,
> but deliver us from the evil one (Matt. 6:13).

Even though it's not pleasant to think about, the reality is all of God's children have a formidable enemy. Satan's goal is to make us sin and to distract us from Christ. He's been lying to mankind since the garden of Eden and he attempts to get us to believe that sin is no big deal, even though the Bible teaches the opposite.

On more than one occasion, the Bible teaches we are to combat the lies of the enemy with prayer and the Word of God.

Christians should be aware but not fearful of the devil because God has already won the ultimate war through the death and resurrection of Jesus. When we pray for God to deliver us from evil, we're reminded that God is all-powerful and that Jesus has already defeated the enemy. As you read the assigned Scriptures this week, ask yourself: What does this passage teach me about God? How does it instruct my prayer life? Am I obeying this Scripture? If not, what changes do I need to make? Journal your answers and reflections.

DAY 1
JOHN 10:10

_____

_____

_____

_____

_____

_____

_____

_____

_____

DAY 3
1 PETER 5:8

_____

_____

_____

_____

_____

_____

_____

_____

_____

DO NOT BRING US INTO TEMPTATION
THE TEMPTATION OF DOUBT

Temptation is as old as the garden of Eden. Although we live in very different times from our first ancestors, the core of our temptations remains the same. At its root, temptation is really about trust. At the heart of every temptation is a simple question that must be answered: Can God really be trusted?

Think back to those first moments in the garden. Everything existed in perfect harmony, and everything worked exactly the way God designed it. There was no want, no dissatisfaction, no unmet expectations, and at the center of all this perfection was an unbroken fellowship between God and humanity. God and His created humans walked together in the garden, fully enjoying one another. Then came the temptation: "Now the serpent was the most cunning of all the wild animals that the Lord God had

made. He said to the woman, "Did God really say, 'You can't eat from any tree in the garden?'" (Gen. 3:1)

The serpent was doing much more than asking the woman a question; he was leveling a charge at the character of God. At the core, then, temptation is not only about our willpower to say yes or no at a given moment, but also about whether we truly believe God loves us and has our best interests in mind when He gives His commands. As you read the assigned Scriptures this week, ask yourself: What does this passage teach me about God? How does it instruct my prayer life? Am I obeying this Scripture? If not, what changes do I need to make? Journal your answers and reflections.

DAY 1
GENESIS 3:1–5

DAY 4
LUKE 24:39-40

_____
_____
_____
_____
_____
_____
_____
_____

DAY 5
JAMES 1:6

_____
_____
_____
_____
_____
_____
_____
_____

DO NOT BRING US INTO TEMPTATION
DEALING WITH DOUBT

If you've been a Christian for any length of time, there's a good chance you've experienced a season of doubt. Perhaps you've wrestled with the truth claims of Christianity or struggled to believe God would come through in a specific circumstance. As human beings, we are prone to doubt and the enemy loves to entice our unbelief. Like Adam and Eve in the garden of Eden, we have a tendency to doubt.

But as believers, we don't have to give in to our doubts. The Bible teaches we are to "rekindle the flame" of our faith (2 Tim. 1:6). The primary way we deal with doubt is by immersing ourselves in the truth of God's Word and praying for God to replace our doubt with faith. We don't have to hide our doubts from God. Scripture is filled with instances of God

ministering to people who were struggling with doubt. When a man with a sick child was struggling to believe Jesus would heal his son, he prayed; "I do believe; help my unbelief!" (Mark 9:29). And Jesus healed his son. As you read the assigned Scriptures this week, ask yourself: What does this passage teach me about God? How does it instruct my prayer life? Am I obeying this Scripture? If not, what changes do I need to make? Journal your answers and reflections.

DAY 1
ROMANS 10:17

_____

_____

_____

_____

_____

_____

_____

_____

_____

_____
_____
_____
_____
_____
_____
_____
_____
_____

_____
_____
_____
_____
_____
_____
_____
_____
_____

DAY 4
JOHN 20:27-29

_____
_____
_____
_____
_____
_____
_____
_____
_____

DAY 5
MATTHEW 21:21

_____
_____
_____
_____
_____
_____
_____
_____
_____

DO NOT BRING US INTO TEMPTATION
THE TEMPTATION BIRTHED

Testing is valuable. Whether in the realm of physical fitness, academic aptitude, or spiritual maturity, tests are valuable for two reasons. First, testing reveals the quality of what's already present in a person. For example, a test in a classroom shows how much knowledge an individual has learned. Second, a test is valuable in developing a person. For example, muscles never develop unless they are regularly tested. Similarly, testing is valuable for our spiritual growth (Jas. 1:2-4).

Only through the testing of our faith do we grow in maturity. This purpose of tests is one God used throughout the Bible and continues to use in our lives today. However, the evil one can corrupt such testing so we need to commit our times of testing to prayer (Jas. 1:13-15).

Although God may allow His people to be tested, He does so only with our good and maturity in mind. But the evil one can take such trials and use them for his wicked purposes. The evil one works with our evil desires to corrupt this opportunity to grow and mature, using it as an opportunity to sin. As we pray for God not to lead us into temptation, we should be aware that temptation doesn't come just from external sources. We need to remain aware of what we're already capable of that arises from our own hearts. As you read the assigned Scriptures this week, ask yourself: What does this passage teach me about God? How does it instruct my prayer life? Am I obeying this Scripture? If not, what changes do I need to make? Journal your answers and reflections.

DAY 1
JAMES 1:2-4

DAY 2
JAMES 1:13-15

_____

_____

_____

_____

_____

_____

_____

_____

_____

DAY 3
LUKE 8:13

_____

_____

_____

_____

_____

_____

_____

_____

_____

DAY 4
2 CORINTHIANS 8:8

_____

_____

_____

_____

_____

_____

_____

_____

_____

DAY 5
HEBREWS 3:8

_____

_____

_____

_____

_____

_____

_____

_____

_____

DO NOT BRING US INTO TEMPTATION
THE TEMPTATION AVOIDED

Faith without action is dead. That is, faith is more than words or a feeling of certainty that God will come through in the end. When we pray, there are other ways besides verbal confirmation to testify that we believe God will respond. When we pray that God won't lead us into temptation but will deliver us from the evil one (see Matt. 6:13), the actions we take reveal the extent to which we trust God to do what we ask. The Scriptures assure us that when we are tempted, God will not allow us to be tempted beyond what we can bear and He will be faithful to provide us a way out of temptation (1 Cor. 10:13). No matter how great our temptation might seem at a given moment, it's common to all humanity. We aren't the first or the last to face such a temptation.

This is where our action connects with our faith as we pray that God won't lead us into temptation but will deliver us from the evil one. The action we need to take is simple: we look for and take the way out that God provides. If we're dealing with temptation by praying and expecting God to simply remove it from our lives, we aren't putting our faith into action. A biblical approach to addressing temptation is to recognize the reality of temptation and not be surprised when it comes. As you read the assigned Scriptures this week, ask yourself: What does this passage teach me about God? How does it instruct my prayer life? Am I obeying this Scripture? If not, what changes do I need to make? Journal your answers and reflections.

DAY 1
1 CORINTHIANS 10:13

_____

_____

_____

_____

_____

_____

_____

_____

_____

DAY 3
GALATIANS 6:1

_____

_____

_____

_____

_____

_____

_____

_____

_____

_____

_____

_____

_____

_____

_____

_____

_____

_____

DAY 5
1 THESSALONIANS 3:5

_____

_____

_____

_____

_____

_____

_____

_____

_____

DO NOT BRING US INTO TEMPTATION
FIGHTING TEMPTATION WITH THE WORD

At its core, temptation is a question of faith. When we're tempted, the root issue is whether God can really be trusted. Does He really love us? Is He really generous? Is He good? Is He really able to provide? Our response to temptation always comes down to our trust in God and His character. Therefore, the way we fight temptation is by reminding ourselves again and again of who God is and then acting accordingly. So, how do we know who God is? Thankfully, we aren't left to speculate about who God is, for He has written it down for us. We know who God is because of His Word.

God's Word is His revelation of Himself. He hasn't left us without a testimony of His will and ways, and He wants us to

know Him. God's Word is the means by which we can know Him. For that reason it's also our weapon for fighting temptation. When Jesus was led into the wilderness to be tempted by Satan, He combatted the enemy by speaking the Word of God (Matt. 4:1-11). God's Word is powerful and of the one the primary tools we should use when dealing with temptation. As you read the assigned Scriptures this week, ask yourself: What does this passage teach me about God? How does it instruct my prayer life? Am I obeying this Scripture? If not, what changes do I need to make? Journal your answers and reflections.

DAY 1
MATTHEW 4:1-4

DAY 2
MATTHEW 4:5-7

_____
_____
_____
_____
_____
_____
_____
_____
_____

DAY 3
MATTHEW 4:8-11

_____
_____
_____
_____
_____
_____
_____
_____
_____

_____

_____

_____

_____

_____

_____

_____

_____

_____

_____

_____

_____

_____

_____

_____

_____

DO NOT BRING US INTO TEMPTATION
FIGHTING TEMPTATION AS PAUL INSTRUCTED

It's easy to forget we are in a spiritual war. The apostle Paul wrote, "For our struggle is not against flesh and blood, but against the rulers, against the authorities, against the cosmic powers of this darkness, against evil, spiritual forces in the heavens" (Eph. 6:12).

In Ephesians 6, Paul described the spiritual armor that's available to every Christian. He described the helmet of salvation, the breastplate of righteousness, the shoes fitted with the gospel of peace, and other defensive pieces of armor. Yet there's only one offensive weapon at our disposal: "the sword of the Spirit—which is the word of God" (Eph. 6:17).

Jesus taught us how to use the sword of God's Word (Matt. 4:1-11). We would do well to look to His example and prepare ourselves for the battles that are inevitably coming our way.

When we pray, then, we ought to pray with the Word of God open. We should pray the promises of God and the statements about His character to Him, knowing that doing so conditions our hand to wield this mighty weapon. As you read the assigned Scriptures this week, ask yourself: What does this passage teach me about God? How does it instruct my prayer life? Am I obeying this Scripture? If not, what changes do I need to make? Journal your answers and reflections.

DAY 1
EPHESIANS 6:10-11

DAY 2
EPHESIANS 6:12

_____

_____

_____

_____

_____

_____

_____

_____

_____

DAY 3
EPHESIANS 6:13-15

_____

_____

_____

_____

_____

_____

_____

_____

_____

_____

_____

_____

_____

_____

_____

_____

_____

DAY 5
EPHESIANS 6:19-20

_____

_____

_____

_____

_____

_____

_____

_____

_____

DO NOT BRING US INTO TEMPTATION
THE TEMPTATION CONQUERED

A conflict rages inside every Christian. When we're born again into Christ, we're made new; we're given a new heart, new tastes, a new identity, and new affections. And yet the old self won't go quietly. An internal battle continues between the flesh and the Spirit of God inside us. It's fought on a myriad of battlefields, both big and small, both visible and invisible. And you know what it feels like. You know the pull of sin. The empty promises of satisfaction. The appeal of desire for immediate gratification. You know the inclinations of the Holy Spirit toward truth, goodness, humility, and holiness. And you know the internal tug-of-war very well. It's conflict in its purest form, and for believers, this conflict is good news.

Consider for a moment what the very presence of that fight inside you means. It means God hasn't given up on you. It means He's committed to making you more like Jesus. It means the Holy Spirit of God is alive and well in you, fighting for your sanctification. It means your faith is real. This fight is painful. This fight is hard. This fight will continue as long as you're on earth. But this fight is good news. But there's even better news to come, for this conflict is temporary. For there will come a day when temptation and the evil one are vanquished. On that day the children of God will see the Lord face-to-face, and all the deepest desires of our souls will be fully realized in Him and in Him alone. As you read the assigned Scriptures this week, ask yourself: What does this passage teach me about God? How does it instruct my prayer life? Am I obeying this Scripture? If not, what changes do I need to make? Journal your answers and reflections.

DAY 1
GALATIANS 5:16–17

_____

_____

_____

_____

_____

_____

_____

_____

_____

DAY 3
ROMANS 8:33-34

_____

_____

_____

_____

_____

_____

_____

_____

_____

DAY 5
ROMANS 8:37-39

Section Eight
REMAINING WATCHFUL

WAITING ON GOD

As we adopt the principles of the Lord's Prayer in our daily prayer life, we need to understand there will be seasons when God calls us to wait on Him. None of us enjoy waiting—we are people who want answers to our prayers. But the Bible shares a long history of God's people waiting for Him to act.

Noah waited out the flood. Abraham waited for an heir. Joseph waited in prison. Hannah waited to become a mother. David waited to take the throne. Daniel waited in exile. Paul waited in prison. There's a biblical precedent of God's people waiting for Him to intervene. We aren't the first, and we won't be the last people who spend time waiting for God to act. As you wait, be encouraged that waiting isn't outside the norm.

Waiting for God to answer our prayers isn't easy, but it's crucial to obey God as we wait. Sometimes when we've been

waiting a long time, there's a temptation to take matters into our own hands, but that's a mistake. David spent years waiting on God before he finally became king of Israel. As David waited, he relied on God's protection, provision, and to fulfill His promise that He would indeed become king. And as David waited, he enjoyed his relationship with God (Ps. 27:4). As you read the assigned Scriptures this week, ask yourself: What does this passage teach me about God? How does it instruct my prayer life? Am I obeying this Scripture? If not, what changes do I need to make? Journal your answers and reflections.

DAY 1
PSALM 27:14

_____

_____

_____

_____

_____

_____

_____

_____

_____

DAY 3
MICAH 7:7

_____

_____

_____

_____

_____

_____

_____

_____

_____

_____
_____
_____
_____
_____
_____
_____
_____
_____

DAY 5
LAMENTATIONS 3:25

_____
_____
_____
_____
_____
_____
_____
_____
_____

STAY ALERT

As Americans, we live in a fast-paced culture. Many of us have packed schedules that keep us rushing from one thing to the next. The responsibilities that come with work, family, homelife, and being an adult demand our attention. On top of that, technology keeps us connected to a constant feed of breaking news, text messages, email, and social media. Now more than ever, we are habitually distracted.

Constant distraction is not conducive to a thriving spiritual life. The Scriptures make it clear that distraction is dangerous. The thoughtful Christian must ask; How is my schedule impacting my relationship with Christ? Am I inclined to skip Bible reading in favor of other activities? Do I spend more time on social media than I do in prayer? Am I prone to check my phone during a worship service? Do I struggle with "being in the moment" because I am distracted?

In the apostle Paul's letter to the Colossians he instructed them, "Devote yourselves to prayer; stay alert in it with thanksgiving" (Col. 4:2). The Christian life calls on us to devote focused time and energy to our prayer lives and to stay watchful. That doesn't mean we should neglect our daily responsibilities—far from it. But it does mean we need to live with intentionality and decide what gets our undivided attention. If our relationship with God is the most important thing then we will be people who devote ourselves to prayer. As you read the assigned Scriptures this week, ask yourself: What does this passage teach me about God? How does it instruct my prayer life? Am I obeying this Scripture? If not, what changes do I need to make? Journal your answers and reflections.

DAY 1
MARK 13:33

_____

_____

_____

_____

_____

_____

_____

_____

_____

DAY 3
PSALM 5:3

_____

_____

_____

_____

_____

_____

_____

_____

_____

_____

_____

_____

_____

_____

_____

_____

_____

DAY 5
LUKE 21:34

_____

_____

_____

_____

_____

_____

_____

_____

OUR FATHER IN HEAVEN,
YOUR NAME BE HONORED AS HOLY.

YOUR KINGDOM COME.
YOUR WILL BE DONE
ON EARTH AS IT IS IN HEAVEN.

GIVE US TODAY OUR DAILY BREAD.

AND FORGIVE US OUR DEBTS.
AS WE ALSO HAVE
FORGIVEN OUR DEBTORS.

AND DO NOT BRING US
INTO TEMPTATION,
BUT DELIVER US
FROM THE EVIL ONE.

MATTHEW 6: 9-13 CSB

PRAYING AT THE CROSSROADS

Learning from the Prayers
of Old Testament Leaders

BIBLE STUDY

GENERAL EDITOR
KEN COLEY